the Rose Quilts

Traditional Applique

The Portable Wrap-Around Method

by
Betty Cossey and Lucille Harrington

Volume One in the
HEIRLOOM SERIES

SMALL CHANGE PRESS
SAN ANSELMO, CALIFORNIA 94960

Copyright ©1993 Betty Cossey and Lucille Harrington

10 9 8 7 6 5 4 3 2 1

All rights reserved. Printed in the United States of America.
No part of this book may be reproduced in any manner, except for brief quotations
in critical articles or reviews, without written permission of the publisher.

Editorial Staff: Judith Keeler, John Parkinson and Jared B. Trace

Art Director: David Paul Turner

Illustrations: David Paul Turner and Lucille Harrington

Typography: Scott Briefer, ARTiculate Communications

Photography: Jon Anderson, Soft Light Photography

Cover: Rose Sampler I has 12 blocks, each a different rose applique pattern. For patterns, see *Chapter Five.*

Applique and quilting: Betty Cossey

If you have any questions or comments concerning this book, please write to:

Small Change Press
524 San Anselmo Avenue, Suite 138
San Anselmo, CA 94960

Cossey, Betty.
   The rose quilts: the portable wrap-around method / Betty
Cossey, Lucille Harrington.
   p. cm.
   ISBN 1-884209-99-8

   1. Quilting – Patterns. 2. Quilts – United States. I.
Harrington, Lucille. II. Title.

TT835.C67 1993   746.46'041
                             QBI93-21684

NOTICE: The authors and editors of this book have tried to make the contents (illustrations, photographs and text) as accurate as possible. However, due to the variability of materials, personal skills, etc., neither the authors nor Small Change Press assumes any responsibility for any damages or other losses incurred that result from the material presented here.

Table of Contents

Acknowledgements

Introduction

Chapter One: Quilting Basics 7

- Supplies and equipment 8
  - Pins 8
  - Needles 8
  - Thimbles 9
  - Scissors 9
  - Paper 9
  - Thread 9
  - Marking pens and pencils 10
  - Templates 11
  - Rulers 11
  - Bias bars 11
  - Hoops 11
  - Pillow 12
- A few words about batting 12
- Fabric 13
  - Color, fabric and imagination 13
  - Choosing fabric 13
  - Preparing fabric 14
  - Direction of fabric 15
- Documenting your quilt 15
- Caring for your quilts 16
  - Washing 16
  - Storing 16
- Displaying quilts 17
  - Create a hanging "sleeve" 17

Chapter Two: Beginning the Quilt 19

- Yardage guidelines 20
- Tracing patterns 20
- Cutting out patterns 21
  - Background fabrics 21
  - Applique pieces 22
- Stitching 24
  - Turn and baste 25
  - Freezer paper technique 26
  - The applique stitch 27
  - Needle turn applique 28
- Finishing 28

Chapter Three: The Portable "Wrap-Around" Method 31
    Overview 32
    Marking quilting 32
    Tearing backing fabric 33
    Cutting/splicing batting 33
    Assembling block for quilting 33
    Quilting 34
    Joining blocks 36
    Preparing and joining borders 37

Chapter Four: Yardage Requirements and Cutting Diagrams 39
    Wallhangings 40
    Three-block Wallhanging 40
    Queen-size quilt 41
    King-size quilt 42

Color Section ....43 – 50
    Rose Sampler I (cover quilt) • Old Rose Quilt • Topeka Rose Quilt • Work-In-Progress
    One-Block Wallhanging • Teddies • Country Dining • Quilt Shop • Rose Sampler II

Chapter Five: The Rose Quilts – Patterns, notes and stitching sequences 51
    Pattern Table 52
    Bud and Rose Wreath (Variation) 53
    Patriot's Rose (Variation) 55
    Rose and Buds 57
    Spring Rose 59
    Country Rose 61
    Harrison Rose 63
    Heartfelt Rose 65
    Circle of Roses 67
    Whig Rose 69
    Rose of Sharon 71
    Rose Wreath 73
    Oregon Rose 75
    Rambling Rose 77
    Rose and Coxcomb 79
    Indiana Rose 81
    Rose and Tulip 83
    Topeka Rose 85
    Ohio Rose 87
    Wild Rose 89
    Forgotten Rose 91
    Border, corner, and heading for "Rose Sampler Quilt I and II" ....93 – 98
    Border, corner, and heading for "Old Rose Quilt" ....99 – 106

Mail Order Sources and Product Information 108

Acknowledgments

Our deepest appreciation to some very special people: Pat Andreatta, for her kind encouragement and gracious permission to use adaptations of her patterns; to Judith Keeler and John Parkinson, for taking a big chance on a small change; to Nancy Eder of Country Lady Quilt Shop in Roseburg, Oregon, for allowing us to use her lovely store for photographing the quilts; to Sally Wheaton of Tolly's "Beckley House" Bed and Breakfast, for her generosity in letting us photograph our quilts in her splendid home.

I would like to thank the following people without whom this book would have been considerably more difficult: To my husband Ken, thank you for all your patience and your help; to my daughter, Sandy Cossey, I deeply appreciate all your assistance and computer knowledge; and to my oldest and dearest quilting buddies, Reba Freeman and Marge Couch, thank you for your encouragement and friendship. And most of all, thank you to Lucille for moving to Oregon and making this book possible.

– *Betty Cossey*

A book is never written in a vacuum and I would like to thank the following people for all that they have done: To my husband Bruce, thank you for your computer expertise and patience; to my family, but especially "Auntie" Carol Plunkett, thank you for your interest and support; to John Parkinson, mere thanks are insufficient to express my feelings – your support and encouragement have been more deeply appreciated than any words can say; to Judith Keeler, a sister is indeed a forever friend, and I'm so glad you're mine.

– *Lucille Harrington*

Introduction

In this book, the beginning stitcher will find the information needed to form a firm foundation in applique technique, and the advanced stitcher will find a new way to approach quilting. And here, all in one place, are 22 patterns; new interpretations of a beloved applique motif – the rose.

Quilts – they hold meaning for each of us. Rarely can a person pass a quilt and not touch it. They stop, stroke the surface for a moment, and then the stories begin; memories of a mother, grandmother, aunt, or perhaps, a dear friend. Although that person may be gone, their love is still visible in the stitches of the quilt, and their memory warms the soul.

Most of us have heirlooms from past generations that link them to us, and we cherish these items for the history that is shared. How lovely to be able to create our own contribution to the future! But, in our busy, hectic lives there doesn't seem to be the small islands of time and space needed to create lovely quilts. Not many houses have the space for a full-sized floor frame or hoop, and our active lifestyles take us out of the home for extended periods of time. How to create a full-sized quilt when we are in the car almost as much as we are in the home? Our generation is perhaps the most mobile since the first man and woman climbed into a covered wagon.

We come, then, to the purpose of this book. Adding your contribution to the history of your family is easier than you may think. Grandmother had to make do with what she had, with what she knew. For us, new products and technical innovations have made some aspects of quilting easier and faster than anyone could have imagined.

Our technique, the portable "wrap-around" method, lets you take your quilting with you, without the need for hoops or frames. It permits you to take advantage of those little pieces of time that fall through the cracks.

So, put some basic quilting supplies into a favorite totebag, add a block or two of your quilt, and leave them in your car. Then, when you find yourself with a few spare moments (waiting for a child to come from school, sitting in a doctor's waiting room, or while stuck in traffic), your work is at hand and easy to pick up. You will be astonished at how much you can accomplish this way!

Before you begin, we make one request. Please don't make beautiful quilts, then tuck them away on a shelf in the closet! Allow them to share your life, hang on your walls and cover your beds. Allow them to become a part of the memories of your family. A child will never know the special warmth of wrapping up in a quilt that was made with love and caring if it is always tucked away in a "safe" place. Share the beauty that love and time can make, and one day, when a member of your family pauses, strokes the surface of a quilt and speaks warmly of the memories that you have created, then you will know that your quilt has truly become an heirloom.

– *Lucille Harrington*

Chapter One

Quilting Basics

Supplies and Equipment
Pins • Needles • Thimbles
Scissors • Paper • Thread
Marking Pens and Pencils
Templates • Rulers • Bias Bars
Hoops • Pillow

A Few Words About Batting

Fabric
Color, Fabric and Imagination
Choosing Fabric • Preparing Fabric
Directions of Fabric

Documenting Your Quilt

Caring for Your Quilts
Washing • Storing

Displaying Quilts
Create a Hanging "Sleeve"

Supplies and Equipment

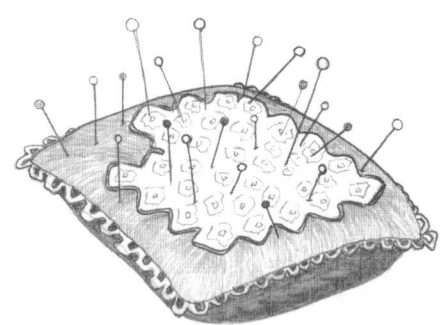

Pins

You will need two different kinds of pins for applique work.

Pinning applique pieces to background fabric

When you are pinning the individual applique pieces to your background fabric, use pins that are thin, sharp, and not too long. Pins that are too long will get in your way and obscure the stitching area. Pins that are too short are awkward to handle and will slow you down.

There are two kinds that we have found to be adequate: ¾" sequin pins, and 1" pleating pins. Experiment to find the length that is most effective for you.

Pins to hold the quilt layers together

When you have finished the applique and are ready to start quilting, you will need a different kind of pin for holding the quilt "sandwich" together. This is a good place for the longest pins you can find. The kind with ball heads work especially well for this purpose. Their length enables you to get a firm grip through all the layers, and the ball heads make it easy to find the pins when you're ready to remove them. (It also makes them easier to find if you drop them on the floor!)

Needles

Most quilters use two different types of needles for their work.

Sharps are used for applique. They are long, slender, and have a relatively small eye. If you are new to quilting, we recommend starting with a size 8 or 9. As you become more comfortable with stitching, you may come to prefer a size 11 or 12; these are the sizes used by most experienced quilters. They are smaller needles and will slide through your fabric more easily.

Betweens are used for quilting. They are shorter, a little "fatter" than sharps, and also have a relatively small eye. (Some brands have a slightly larger eye than other brands, making them a little easier to thread.) We recommend that the new stitcher start off with a size 8 or 9. As you become more proficient at hand-quilting, the shorter sizes of 10 and 12 will enable you to make more uniform, smaller stitches.

Since some quilters prefer using betweens instead of sharps for their applique work, you might want to experiment to find the most comfortable needle and size. Until you know which you prefer, needles in assorted sizes in one package are a convenient way to experiment.

Many quilters prefer English needles when they are available. We are particularly fond of *John James Needles* or *S. Thomas & Sons Needles*, but there are many other brands that are also good. The best ones are the ones that suit you!

There are two things to remember about both sharps and betweens. The higher the number of the needle, the smaller it is. And, the smaller the needle, the smaller the stitches can be.

Chapter One: Quilting Basics

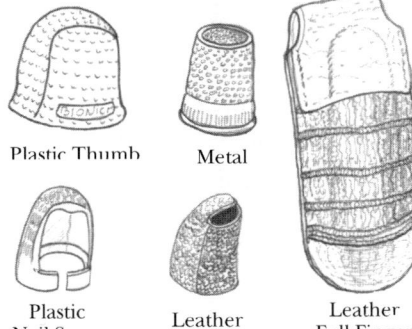

Plastic Thumb   Metal

Plastic Nail Saver   Leather   Leather Full Finger

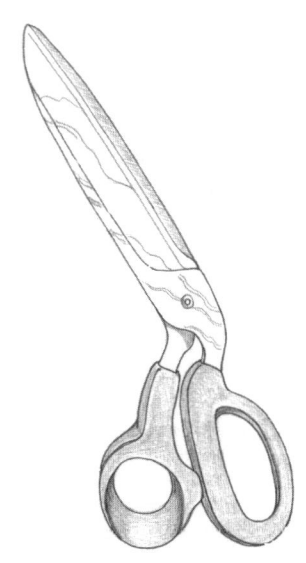

Thimbles

A discussion of needles is a good place for a discussion of thimbles. Even if you have never used a thimble before, quilting is a great time to start.

If you have worn a thimble in the past and found it to be uncomfortable, we encourage you to give it another try. It will mean more to your quilting (and to your finger!) than you can imagine. There are many different styles of thimbles on the market, and what works well for one quilter may not suit another. Buy a variety and give each a good honest trial until you find the right one. When you do, buy at least two of them. Don't waste good quilting time looking for a thimble that has temporarily misplaced itself.

With time and a little practice, a good thimble will become so much a part of your quilting routine that you'll find it hard to believe you ever stitched without one.

Scissors

You will need several pairs of scissors for different uses. Reserve your best pairs of scissors for cutting fabric only. When cutting the fabric pieces of the applique design, we recommend using a smaller pair of scissors to make the work easier and more comfortable.

For cutting paper, cardboard or template plastic, however, do not use your good fabric-cutting scissors, as this dulls scissors very quickly. Dull scissors can cause unwanted ragged or tattered edges on the fabric.

Paper

For making placement guides for the applique design, you will need several sheets of 8½" x 11" paper. Use any lightweight white paper that is transparent enough to see the design through.

If you would prefer a more permanent pattern, consider using lightweight, transparent interfacing (non-woven material), such as *Do-Sew*.

Thread

For applique work, good-quality, all-purpose sewing thread in colors to match the applique fabric works well. Many quilters prefer all-cotton thread or cotton-covered polyester when sewing cotton fabrics, but we've found that polyester thread is just fine, too.

If you have a print, and are unsure about which color to match, pick the color that is most predominant at the edge of the pattern piece, inside the seam allowance, as this is where you will be stitching. If it is difficult to match the exact shade, always choose a thread that is a shade darker, rather than a shade lighter.

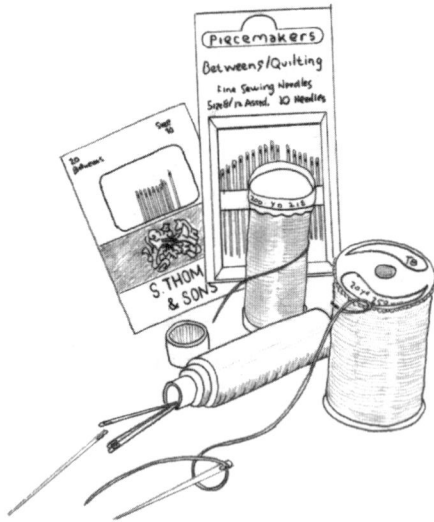

For quilting, special "hand-quilting" thread should be used. It is a slightly heavier weight, is usually 100% cotton and frequently comes from the manufacturer with a glaze to make it easier to handle, less likely to tangle and knot and give bettter wear over the life of the quilt. After all the work you will put into your lovely piece, don't skimp on this detail; hand-quilting thread is inexpensive and it does make a difference.

Marking Pens and Pencils

There is a dazzling array of marking devices on the market, and the right one for the right job makes your work so much smoother. Here are some that we recommend.

A blue, water-soluble marking pen, such as *Mark-B-Gone* or *Wonder Marker*, is our choice for marking placement guides on the background fabric. You may also use it for tracing individual applique pieces on lighter fabrics.

When the stitching is complete, spray the marked fabric with cold water, blot with a paper towel, and the blue pen marks will completely disappear. If they reappear when the fabric dries, don't panic – simply repeat the spraying and blotting. This sometimes occurs with a new pen; they can be a bit "juicy." In rare instances, the ink may not completely disappear from the fabric. Be sure to take notice of the caution printed on the back of the packaging and to be on the safe side, test the water-soluble pen on a scrap of fabric before using it on your quilt.

There is a purple, air-soluble marking pen (*Disappearing Ink Marking Pen*) that is also useful. Air-soluble means is that the marks made with this pen will disappear by themselves or with water. Depending on the humidity of the particular day that you use the pen, the marks can last anywhere from a few hours to a day or two.

Please don't confuse the blue marking pen with the purple marking pen – they are not simply different colors of ink!

Please don't confuse the blue marking pen with the purple marking pen – they are not simply different colors of ink! Nothing is more frustrating than spending time and effort to mark quilting or placement lines that you expect to be permanent, and finding a blank piece of fabric staring at you later!

For tracing around applique pieces that will be stitched down onto the fabric, use any type of marking that will not disappear, is visible against the fabric, and does not leave oil traces. Light chalk pencils are very good against darker fabrics, and the blue pen, *Mark-B-Gone,* may be just what's needed for the light fabrics. When using any marking pencil or pen, use a light hand and do not press down hard.

Quilting lines are frequently drawn with a #2 lead pencil or mechanical pencil with a .5mm lead. There is a new .5mm mechanical pencil on the market designed just for quilters that works particularly well. The lines should be visible enough to stitch, but not any darker than absolutely

Chapter One: Quilting Basics

necessary. If you wish, you could use the blue marking pen, *Mark-B-Gone*, or a *Wonder Marker* here as well.

Templates

Thin plastic (sometimes called template plastic) is readily available at quilt shops and most fabric stores, and is excellent for making applique templates. You can see through it to place the motifs on the fabric in just the desired position. It also has the advantage of not wearing down with repeated use.

You will need cardboard, too, for making circles. Any clean, lightweight cardboard will do. Clean cereal boxes, cracker boxes, and poster board are all good sources. Look around – you probably have something on hand that will work just fine.

Rulers

You will need something to help you measure the background fabric and the backing. Any type of ruler that is see-through will be excellent, and there are many brands and sizes on the market.

Bias bars

The metal and nylon bias bars that are on the market are just great! Buy them individually, or in sets of assorted sizes. They are needed to make the stems on any applique project.

For all the blocks in this book, we have used the ¼" bias bar. Two quilters who have designed bias bars are Pat Andreatta (*Bias Press Bars* from *Heirloom Stitches*) and Philomena Durcan (*Bias Bars* from *Celtic Design Company*). (See the "*Mail Order Sources*" section in this book for information on finding these products.)

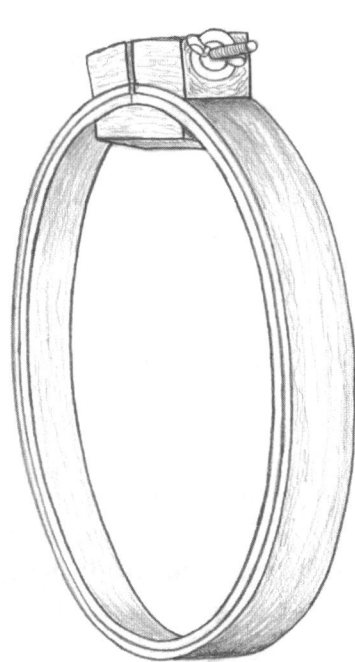

Hoops

To hoop or not to hoop?

This is a question guaranteed to start a spirited discussion in any group of quilters. You will find as many devotees of the hoop as you will find detractors, and it is an entirely personal decision.

We don't feel there is any necessity for a hoop during the applique stitching, and our portable, wrap-around method is particularly good for quilting without a hoop.

Many quilters turn out beautiful work without their quilts ever touching a hoop or frame. If, however, you have a tendency to pull the stitches tight enough to cause distortion, a hoop will prevent that. Try quilting

with and without a hoop, and see what is most comfortable for you. There is no right or wrong way, just your way!

Pillow

Pillows are not just to sleep on. A thick, lightweight pillow on your lap when appliqueing or quilting will bring the work closer and save you from bending over and straining your back and shoulders. By resting your forearms on the pillow as you stitch, your shoulders can relax, and you can work for longer periods of time with less strain.

And, since the pillow is right there in front of you, pin your applique pieces to it. Then, as you need them, they are there at your fingertips.

A Few Words About Batting

The batting is the middle layer of the quilt "sandwich," and gives your piece that beautiful sculptured look. It is important to use a good quality product, and one that is easy to "needle." For hand-quilting, polyester batting is the easiest.

If you are buying batting by the yard, 3-ounce polyester is a good, standard weight to use for quilting the applique blocks. It is easy to work with, gives good definition to your quilting stitches, and is readily available in most quilt and fabric stores.

Cotton batts give a flatter, more traditional look. If you choose to use cotton batting, be aware that most are extremely difficult to hand-quilt through, and are best left for the machine quilter. Unless they are preshrunk according to the directions on the wrapper, they can shrink considerably when the quilt is washed for the first time.

Extra loft batts, although softer than cotton, are also more difficult for hand-quilting. The extra fiber in the batt makes it hard on the hand, and these are best for tied comforters, as they make up into a soft and "poofy" piece.

The rule of thumb is: The thicker the batt, the longer your stitches will be. The thinner the batt, the smaller your stitches can be.

Keep in mind that the thicker the batting, the more difficult it is to achieve small, even stitches. Although small stitches were the standard by which old quilts were measured, it was pretty easy for them to do. Their batts were quite thin, so it was not too difficult to sew 12 stitches to the inch. What matters most, however, is not how small your stitch is, but how consistent and even.

If you have found the local quilt shop, this would be a good place to look for batting. If you have any doubts about which product to use, ask them for advice. Some mail-order catalogs will allow you to order swatches of each type of batting that they sell, and this is a good way to check out what is available on the market.

Chapter One: Quilting Basics

Fabric

The most important thing to remember is that color taste is totally subjective! It doesn't matter if no one else in the world likes the colors you have chosen. If those colors "speak" to you and make your heart joyful just to look at them, then you have chosen well, and you will always feel a special fondness for that quilt.

Color, Fabric and Imagination

What is the first thing that you notice about a quilt? Before you recognize the pattern, before you admire the fine stitching, you see the colors.

For some quilters, choosing colors and fabric is the most difficult part of the quilting-making process. For others, it's their cup of tea, and this section is not for those lucky souls. It is, instead, for those of us who tend to agonize over our color selections. So, if you hit a blank wall on color choice, here are a few little tricks that quilters have used over the years.

First, find a print that attracts your eye. Open it out on the counter, and look at it carefully. Notice the colors that make up the print, and start "pulling" them out. Perhaps your choice is a floral. Look at the individual flowers to really see the colors of each one. Then go back to the shelves and find a solid, or maybe a small print fabric, in those colors. Repeat with other colors in the print until there is a working palette of colors in a variety of fabrics.

By pulling the colors out from a print, you can easily incorporate several fabrics into your quilt, and can be assured that all the colors will blend well.

The other technique is to simply open your mind to seeing color combinations everywhere around you.

As you admire beautiful flowering shrubs and flowers in the spring, notice that Mother Nature puts colors together in ways that mere mortals would never imagine. Take a cue from the riotous way nature combines colors and free yourself from color limits. Notice the different shades of green, distinguish the different colors of flowers. In a floral arrangement, what colors and shades appeal to you most? Sometimes you can develop a color scheme from that. Inspiration is all around us. As with fabric, "pull" colors from whatever particularly strikes you.

Remember, it isn't possible to please everyone with what you choose. It is only important that you are happy with your choices. There is no right or wrong in any aspect of quilting, and color choice is no exception.

Choosing Fabric

After you've decided on a color scheme, it is time to consider the actual materials that you will be using to make your quilt. Our ancestors were more likely to use whatever they had at hand, but we have far more choices now.

Cotton, especially 100% cotton, is the easiest fabric with which to work. Although some blends of cotton and polyester may be just the perfect color and seem to have a nice weight, you will not know until you actually cut and start to stitch whether they will work well in your piece. We also recommend that you avoid any fabric that has even a small amount of

rayon fiber (rayon is difficult to work with, as it can shrink, wrinkle and/or fray).

Until you are very comfortable with your ability to choose fabrics that will handle well, we strongly recommend that you choose 100% cottons for your quilt. Cotton stitches beautifully, washes well, and will not fight you as can other fabrics.

Fortunately, with the renewed interest and appreciation of handwork, it is not the task it once was to find good quality cottons in a wide range of colors. If you are lucky enough to have a good quilt shop in your area, we suggest you go in and introduce yourself to the clerks. It is so nice to find people who are willing to let you take out bolt after bolt of fabric, and then cheerfully cut ¼ yard pieces of 20 different fabrics.

For the backgrounds of the blocks, if you are looking for a natural color, consider good old unbleached muslin. There have been big improvements in the production of this favored standby. If you need a whiter fabric, you have the choice of buying bleached muslin or, if you already have a nice stash of unbleached muslin lying around, add chlorine bleach to the wash water and create your own white fabric. Muslin is so very nice to stitch on, and it quilts beautifully. You can, however, use whatever fabric you like.

Preparing Fabric

All fabric must be preshrunk by washing before you begin, or you can have an unhappy surprise the first time your quilt is cleaned.

Cotton fabrics should be washed in the same water temperature that will be used to wash the quilt in the future. Use a good but gentle soap, and wash similar colors together. Since you are using several colors in your quilt, you do not want to find out that the red fabric still runs after it's in the same wash water as the pale yellow fabric.

It is not enough to simply place the fabric in the washer and come back when the cycle is through. With all fabrics, but with red and dark colors especially, it is important to check the color of the water during the wash cycle, and again during the rinse cycle. If there is color in the water in either cycle, wash the fabrics again, and check the water as before. If there continues to be noticeable coloration of the water, seriously consider replacing the fabric. Some things are not worth fooling with, and fabric that is not colorfast is one of them.

All fabrics in the store have sizing that was added by the manufacturer. It gives the fabric a firmer hand, and allows for easier processing by the maker. You do want this excessive sizing to be washed out, but you do not want the fabric to be too soft. It is just about perfect when it comes from the washer and dryer with no fabric softener added. There will be a

Chapter One: Quilting Basics

good handling body to the material, and this will aid you immeasurably while stitching.

So do not add liquid fabric softener to the rinse water, and do not use the fabric softener strips that are placed into the dryer. Many dark fabrics will come from the dryer with streaks that are caused by these strips, so take no chances with your fabrics. Just give them a good wash, a quick dry, and get to the fun.

Direction of Fabric

All things that are visible reflect light.

Now, I know you may be wondering why this tidbit of information is included in a quilting book, but the point is that fabric reflects light. And this explains why a quilt will look one way when viewed from one angle, and may look different when viewed from another angle.

If, when cutting the pieces for your applique, you do not cut them all in the same direction, you may find that they each reflect light differently. Depending on the fabric and the color, this could detract quite noticeably from the beauty of the quilt.

A good way to illustrate what we are talking about is to take a good look at corduroy. Now, you would never use this heavy napped fabric in a quilt, but it demonstrates exactly what we are discussing here. Corduroy has a nap and reflects light very differently according to the direction of the nap. When the nap is running down, the reflection of light is greatest, and the color of the fabric will appear lighter and even slightly shiny or "frosted." When the nap is running up, there is less light reflected and the color of the material is distinctly different (darker), and there is no sheen. When garment sewing with corduroy, if you should accidentally change the direction of the fabric while cutting, nothing will correct the way the garment will appear when sewn. No matter how beautifully constructed, the distinct color difference will catch the eye and everything else will be secondary.

Cotton fabrics are far more subtle than corduroy, but the fact remains, be very careful when cutting your pieces, because...all things that are visible reflect light!

Documenting Your Quilt

Even though your beautiful quilt is finished, you are not quite done.

Handwork (and quilts especially) become more valuable with the passage of time. When finished with your work, sign and date it on the back, or on the front in a small block if the backing fabric is a busy floral which obscures your writing.

If the quilt is being given as a gift to commemorate a special occasion or a special person, note that on the quilt as well. And be sure to use your full name – years from now there may be more than one person in your family with the same first name, and it will be of great interest to those who come after to know exactly who it was that took the time to create such a lovely legacy.

There are many ways to put this information on your quilt. You can write carefully with one of the new pens that are designed for fabric use. They do not bleed and are permanent. They come in a lovely assortment of colors and are quick and easy to use.

If you prefer, cross-stitch a label that will be stitched to the back, or write the information on a piece of muslin, and applique it to your work. There are several terrific books on the market that illustrate many different techniques of documenting your work, as well as demonstrating some of the ways that older quilts were documented.

Quilt historians always look for as much information as possible on the quilt itself, and the value of a quilt will rise with the level of documentation. Although you may plan for your quilt to remain in your family line forever, it is still highly recommended that you provide as much data as you can. You are, after all, telling future generations why you made this beautiful heirloom, and for whom it was intended. You are documenting your family legacy, and linking your life to theirs.

Caring For Your Quilts

Washing

Light vacuuming while the piece is hanging will take care of most dust problems. If, however, the piece should require more thorough cleaning, it may be dry cleaned, or washed in a double or triple-sized (extra-large size) tumble washer found in most laundromats. These have more room, and are more gentle to a quilt than the average home agitator washer. Use warm water and detergent without bleach, or if you prefer, *Orvus Quilt Soap*. This product is extremely gentle and is used by many textile historians to launder antique quilts.

To dry your piece, place it in a large dryer, using gentle heat until it is almost dry. Lay it out on a flat surface or bed to complete the drying process. Again, avoid direct exposure to sunlight.

Storing

If your work is to be stored, avoid folding it as creases will form which may become permanent. Wrap a cardboard tube (such as a paper towel or wrapping paper core) with acid-free tissue paper. Place at one end of the piece and roll it around the core into a tube shape. Wrap the outside

Chapter One: Quilting Basics

in acid-free tissue paper, or, if you prefer, fabric such as a sheet or pillowcase. If the quilt is too large to comfortably handle in this way, folding may be unavoidable. If that is the case, open the quilt from time to time to air it and refold it differently.

Never place quilted items in plastic bags. Plastic does not "breathe," and any slight moisture trapped in the bag may cause mildewing which could leave permanent stains and cause deterioration of the fabric. With minimal care, a quilted piece will last for many, many, years.

Displaying Quilts

However you decide to display quilted items, never hang them or place them where the sunlight will shine directly onto the fabric. This promotes premature fading, and over a longer period of time will cause deterioration of the fabric called "sun rot."

Create a Hanging "Sleeve"

To finish your wallhanging, sew a "sleeve" on the back for hanging. A sleeve is a tube of fabric that is sewn onto the back at the top of the piece.

To hang your quilted work, insert a dowel rod into the sleeve, making sure it extends past each end of the sleeve. The rod is then hung from whatever hanging devices you desire. A slight rippling of the edges of the quilted piece is normal, and in most cases, unavoidable.

After the piece is hung, straight pins inserted through the hanging into the wall will allow the piece of hang evenly. Straight pins will not damage the fabric, but DO NOT USE NAILS! They will permanently damage the quilt.

Chapter Two

Beginning the Quilt

Yardage Guidelines

Tracing Patterns

Cutting Out Patterns
Background Fabrics
Applique Pieces

Stitching
Turn and Baste
Freezer Paper Technique
The Applique Stitch
Needle Turn Applique

Finishing

Yardage Guidelines

Here are some general guidelines about yardage. (Specific yardage requirements for each quilted project is given in *Chapter Four: Yardage Requirements and Cutting Diagrams.*)

These wrap-around quilts do best with a multi-colored backing fabric. A non-directional floral is the easiest to use. It is the back of the quilt and will be the sashing between the blocks. Use some of this fabric in each block and add three or four colors for the flowers. These colors can be "pulled" from the print of the main fabric. For the flowers, use solids, prints, or a combination of both.

If you prefer, use the same fabric for the back and the background of the blocks on the front. This eliminates the contrasting sashes and gives a whole-cloth look to the front.

Tracing Patterns

First of all, feel free to change any pattern, in this book or in any other. If you don't like a bud, leaf, or flower, change it! If you like the pattern, but not the leaf, for example, find one you do like, and use that. We like five-petaled flowers and often use them in place of a one-piece flower, but the reverse could be used just as easily. If you would prefer a different border, try a vine.

Just be sure to place the flowers or leaves on the stems so that you will not have to make any seams in the bias fabric. You can also avoid seams in the bias fabric by making bias strips that are long enough for a particular stem length.

For tracing our patterns, we recommend using sheets of lightweight, transparent 8½" x 11" paper. Our patterns are given in "sections" that will easily fit onto that size paper.

Depending on the pattern, trace each pattern "section" onto a separate 8½" x 11" sheet of paper one or more times. (Refer to *Chapter Five: The Rose Quilts – Patterns, Notes and Stitching Sequences.*) The patterns will tell you how many times to trace each section, and then show you how the pattern sections should look when they are joined together to form the whole design.

After you have traced the pattern onto the paper and joined it together (with tape on the back), go over the design again with a black permanent marker. You now have a full 18" pattern to be used for applique or, if you choose, as a quilting design. (Please note: As all applique patterns in this book are hand-drawn, some adjustment may be necessary for pattern lines to meet.)

To prepare the border or heading patterns, trace and join the patterns as directed in *Chapter Five: The Rose Quilts – Patterns, Notes and Stitching Sequences.* The borders have a 20" repeat and will fit directly above or

Chapter Two: Beginning The Quilt

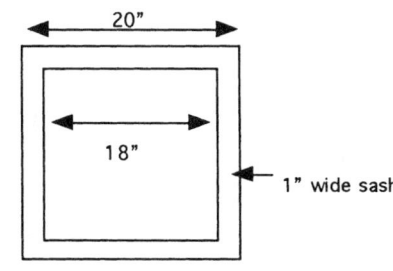

Dimensions of finished block

below each 20" block. (Each block measures 20" x 20" after the sashing is stitched down. The interior measurement of each block is 18" x 18", and the sashing measures 1" on each side).

Any lightweight, non-fusible interfacing material (such as *Do-Sew*) could be used instead of paper for the patterns. It does not tear as easily as paper, and makes a good permanent pattern for future use.

Using a piece of interfacing large enough to fit the whole design (20" x 10" for borders and headings, and 18" square for all other patterns), trace the pattern with a pencil, then go over it with a black felt-tipped pen. (Ink from felt-tipped pens will penetrate through interfacing quite readily, so protect the surface on which you are working with newspaper or cardboard.) When you are ready to trace the pattern onto the background fabric of the block, place the pattern on a light-colored surface. You can then center the fabric and trace the pattern easily with a water-soluble marking pen.

You will need lightweight cardboard or plastic to make templates for the applique pieces. If you use plastic, simply place the sheet over your placement guide and trace off the various pieces with a permanent marker. It helps to number the various pieces on the placement guide, and use those same numbers as you trace off the patterns. If you are using cardboard, trace your pattern pieces onto a separate sheet of paper, cut out, and glue to cardboard. Again, number the individual pieces. Cut all pieces exactly as they are drawn; do not add seam allowances now.

This is a good time to note on the pattern pieces which edges will go under another section of the applique. This is important, because you need the seam allowances under the next piece, but you do not want the bulk of a turned and stitched down edge. Dotted lines show up well on plastic or cardboard, and are a signal to you as you cut out that this edge will not be turned, but will lie flat. You do, however, need to add the same seam allowance that you would to all the other edges.

For making circles, cut templates out of cardboard. (You will see why a little later when we describe the actual cutting of the fabric.)

Store all of the template pieces in plastic zip-type bags. Be sure to write the name of the pattern on the outside.

Cutting Out Patterns

Background fabrics

In preparing background fabrics, we recommend that you tear them. Tearing your fabric into the size you need, instead of cutting, will give exact grainlines, minimize puckering and stretching, making your work easier and your finished quilt hang or lie beautifully.

To tear the fabric, first make a snip through the selvage at one end and tear across the width of it. Snip through the selvage at the other side. Measure for the background blocks from the torn edge. Follow the cutting diagrams carefully for maximum use of your fabric, and repeat the same process for all the sections required for your project.

Be sure to mark the top of each block in the seam allowance before separating it from the main fabric. This is very important because fabric reflects light (see "*Direction of fabric,*" page 15.) If, when you cut the pieces for the applique, you do not cut them all in the same direction, they each may reflect light differently. Depending on the fabric and the color, this could detract quite noticeably from the beauty of your quilt.

If you forget to mark your blocks, try "stretching" each block. Fabric is very stable on the lengthwise grain, but will have a little "give" on the crosswise grain. This stretch test will help keep all the blocks going in the same direction!

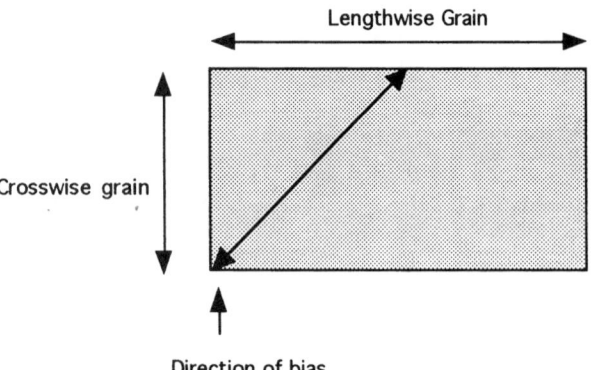

Using small pieces of masking tape, fasten the pattern to a light-colored, firm, smooth surface. Crease the background fabric to mark the center and place it over the center mark on the pattern. The fabric will be larger than the pattern; fasten it to the surface with small pieces of masking tape, as well.

If the pattern does not show through the fabric clearly, make a "light table." Place a small lamp under any table with a glass top, and have the light shine up through the fabric. If no glass-topped tables are available, tape the pattern and fabric to a window, and do your tracing there.

Trace the pattern onto your fabric LIGHTLY, using a water-soluble marking pen, such as *Mark-B-Gone* or *Wonder Marker*. Set the traced fabric to one side, and begin to cut out the applique pieces.

Applique Pieces

With applique, everything is marked on the right side (front) of the fabric. The templates are the finished size, with no seam allowances added,

Chapter Two: Beginning The Quilt

for you will add the seam allowances as you cut. Again, make sure all the applique pieces are cut with the grainlines in the same direction.

Using a light hand and a sharp pencil or water-soluble pen such as *Mark-B-Gone* or *Wonder Marker*, trace around each pattern piece, allowing ¼" seam allowance on all sides, and being sure to allow ½" between pieces.

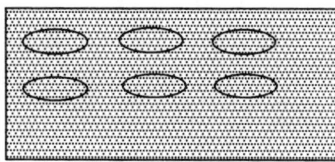 It is always better to err on the side of allowing too much space between pieces than too little. Notice, too, that all the pieces are laid out in the same direction.

Cut out pieces, adding the ¼" seam allowance as you cut. If your seam allowance is not an absolute, true ¼", that's all right. You just want to allow enough fabric to turn under.

As you cut, note which pieces have the "dotted" edges, and make a little mark on those sides; keep the marks in the seam allowance where they will not show. These are edges that will go under another piece, and it is handy to have a visual marker.

When cutting out circles, mark in the same way as the other applique pieces, but allow a little more than a ¼" seam allowance. To form the circles, take small running stitches around the circle, about ⅛" in from the edge. Place the cardboard template inside the circle of fabric, and draw the threads taut. The fabric will pull into the center. Holding the threads firmly, steam with an iron, then allow to cool. Carefully loosen the stitches enough to remove the cardboard template, then pull the threads back up to bring the fabric back into the pressed shape. You should have a perfect circle, ready to applique.

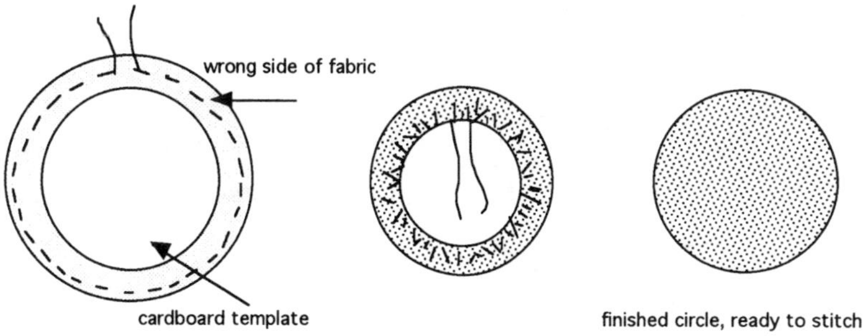

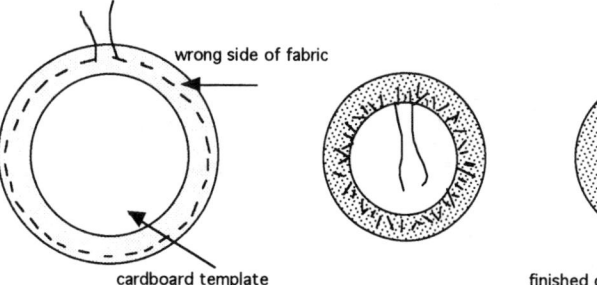

cardboard template — finished circle, ready to stitch

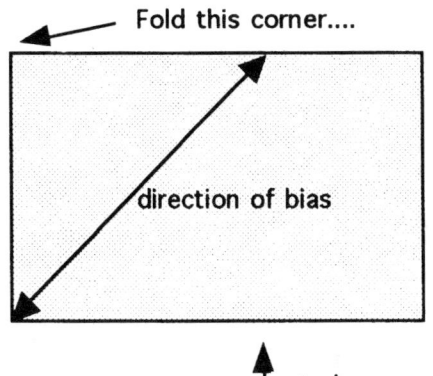

Fold this corner....
direction of bias
....to here

To make stems for your project, cut strips on the bias (diagonal) of the fabric. The bias has the most stretch, and will curve beautifully wherever needed. To find the true bias, either use a ruler that has a 45° marking, or fold the upper left corner of the fabric down until the left vertical edge of the fabric aligns with the bottom. The fold is the true bias.

If you have metal or nylon bias bars, follow the directions given by the manufacturer. If using the metal bias bars, be careful – they can get hot when you steam-press. If you don't have bias bars available, make your own from a piece of thin, rigid cardboard. The cardboard "bias bar" should measure ¼" wide by about 12" long.

Cut the fabric on the bias into strips that are ⅞" wide. Short pieces are fine; there is no need to sew strips together. Fold the strips in half and sew wrong sides together by hand or machine, as close to the cut edges as possible. This will form a tube. Slide the bias bar into the tube, centering the seam in the middle, and steam press. Remove the bar, and your stems are ready.

Stitching

You are ready to stitch now! Your background fabric is prepared, your pieces are cut, and now... where do you start?

For ease in appliqueing, we have numbered our patterns to show the sequence in which parts of the design should be stitched. For instance, the leaves will be marked with L1, L2, L3, etc., showing the order in which to stitch the leaves (L = leaves). The flowers will be marked with F1, F2, F3, etc. (F = flowers).

If you are using patterns other than ours, there may not be any stitching guides to follow. Here, then, is how to analyze a pattern and determine the best stitching sequence.

Generally speaking, applique designs are stitched from the background of the design to the front. In other words, first find the portion of the pattern that will be *under* other segments of the design.

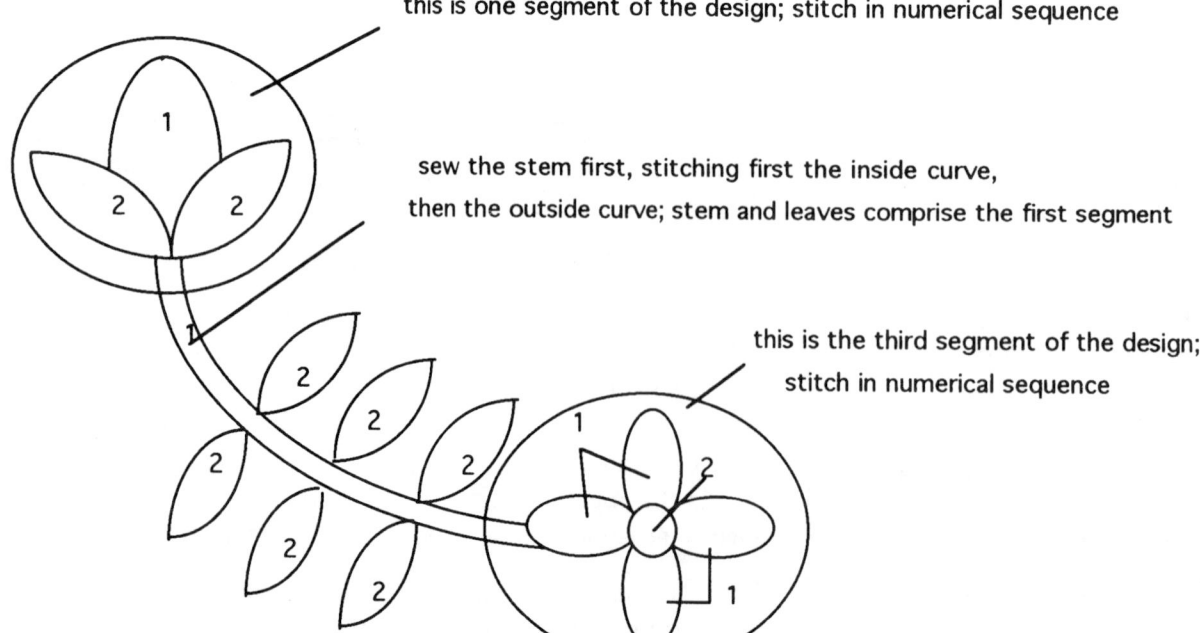

Chapter Two: Beginning The Quilt

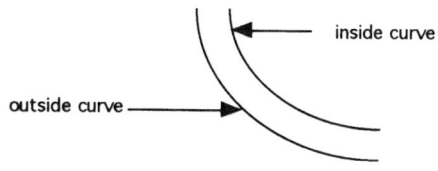

In this design, the stem would be stitched first because it is behind both the flower at the bottom and the bud and leaves at the top. It is the most "background" element of the design. When stitching the stem, sew down the inside curve first; the outside curve will then lie beautifully flat.

Be sure to have the stem ends extend ¼" into the flower segment and ¼" into the bud and leaf segment, as well. After the stems are in place, you are ready to stitch down the other portions of the design.

All the leaves along the stem are numbered the same. Since none of them go behind the stem, but just touch along the outer edges, they can be done as you choose, although I would suggest stitching from top to bottom.

You may then stitch either the "flower" segment, or the "bud and leaves" segment next.

Following the sequence for the bud and leaves, you can see that the bud (1) is behind the two leaves (2). This is when the dotted marks on the applique piece come in handy; the outer edges of bud (1) will be stitched down, but where it will be covered by the leaves, you will simply allow these edges to extend into the leaf portion. The leaves (either the left or the right) will be stitched around all sides, and the opposite leaf will just touch at the center point.

The flower portion at the bottom will be stitched in the same way. Where the petals of the flower will be covered by the circle in the middle, this fabric will be allowed to lie flat. The circle would then cover all raw edges in the middle.

There are several ways to applique, but there are three techniques that we recommend:

- *turn and baste applique*
- *freezer paper technique*
- *needle-turn applique*

Turn and Baste

For the beginner, we would suggest turning and basting to be an especially effective method.

Holding the applique piece with the wrong side facing you, roll the seam allowance toward you with your thumb until you can see the marked line. Roll just a little more until the pencil line is on the back (this prevents it from being visible from the right side). Baste the seam allowance with small running stitches that are as close to the edge as possible.

Inside curves will require some clipping so that they will lie flat, but outside curves, unless they are very sharp, should fold without any difficulty. If it is necessary to clip, stop just short of the marked line.

To make sharp points, follow the directions below:

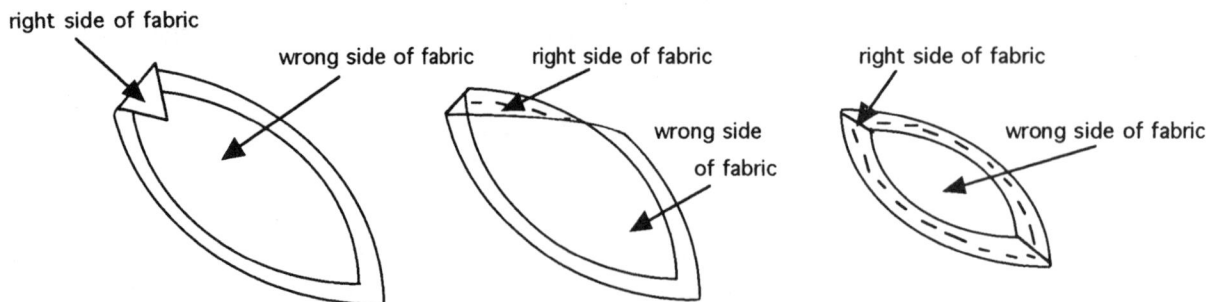

Fold tip down to the marked seam allowance.   Fold one side over, and baste.   Continue basting and fold other tip. Baste.

Another place that needs some special attention is at inward points. These must be clipped in order to turn them.

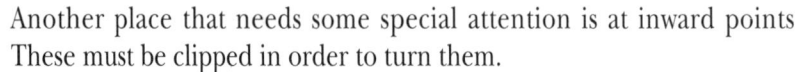

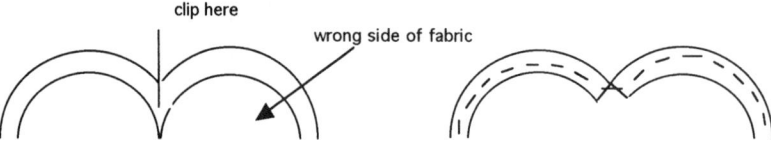

Clip to just before the seam allowance line, and baste the edge down as shown. (This applies regardless of the applique technique used.)

Freezer Paper Technique

Sometimes, it is difficult to find an effective marker for a multi-colored print. One may show up well on the dark sections, but is lost in the light areas, or vice versa. To avoid this frustration, we recommend using the freezer paper technique.

Freezer paper is found in the wrap section of the supermarket. There are several brands, but you want the poly-coated white paper that you would use to wrap meats or other items for the freezer, such as *Reynolds Freezer Paper*.

Trace off onto the paper (the non-shiny side) as many copies of the pattern piece as you need for the design, and cut them out. You will now have several freezer-paper "patterns." With a hot iron, iron the freezer paper patterns (shiny side down) to the RIGHT side of your fabric, allowing for seam allowances.

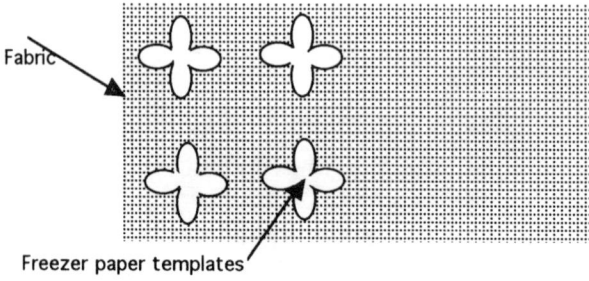

Chapter Two: Beginning The Quilt

Cut out the patterns, with the seam allowances, and carefully pin the unit (made of the fabric and the freezer paper) to the appropriate place on the background fabric. It helps to align specific points. If you are working on a leaf, for example, put a pin through the top point, and insert this same pin through the corresponding point on the background fabric. Align the bottom the same way, and pin securely.

Note: When pinning, you do not want slippage of the two layers of fabric, so "stab" the applique piece straight down, not at an angle, hold both fabrics together firmly, then turn the pin to secure the pieces.

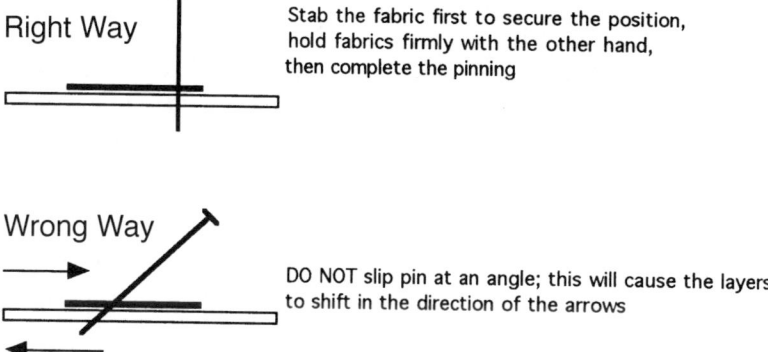

After placing the applique in its proper place, you will then use the "needle turn technique" and the applique stitch to complete your stitching. After all stitching is complete, remove the freezer paper. (If you remove it carefully, you might be able to reuse it!)

The Applique Stitch

Coming from behind the background fabric, bring your needle straight up through the background fabric and the folded edge of the applique piece. Keep your stitches as close to the edge as possible. Go straight out from this first stitch, and under the applique piece just a little bit. While the tip of your needle is in the fabric, angle it to your left (if you are right-handed), and come up through the fold of the applique piece again. Use a sewing motion, rather than a "stab and pull" motion. Keep the stitches fairly close together; a little practice will help achieve the proper spacing.

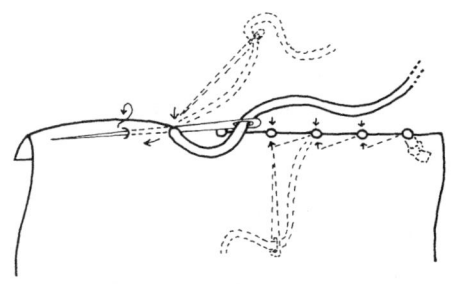

When you reach the end of the line of stitching, take the thread to the back of the piece, and secure it with a knot. If you are using a darker thread than your background fabric color, be sure that all knots (beginning and ending) are under the applique to avoid thread "tails" that can be seen through the fabric. That's all there is to it! Continue appliqueing all pieces until the design is complete.

Needle Turn Applique

This is the third technique that we recommend, and the one that most experienced stitchers use. It takes a little practice to become completely comfortable with it, but it is well worth the effort.

Prepare the applique pieces in the same way as in the "turn and baste" technique (trace around the templates on the right side of the fabric, allowing plenty of space for seam allowances, then cut out. Pin into the proper position as outlined above in the freezer paper technique and secure with as many pins as are needed.)

Start stitching on the straightest (least curved) portion of the applique piece. Gently turn the seam allowance under with the tip of the needle until the marked line is underneath. Placing the thumb of your opposite hand on this folded edge, bring the knotted thread from behind the background fabric or from under the applique piece itself. Take a stitch to secure, then stitch close to the edge of the applique (using the applique stitch shown above) until you can go no further.

At that point, turn under the next section to stitch, hold with your thumb, and continue sewing. Be sure not to leave threads too loose at the edge of the applique, which is a common mistake. The threads should "fuse" with your fabric – snug the edges down as firmly as possible without causing any puckering or dimpling of the fabrics. Continue working around the applique piece, clipping any areas that require it to allow the edge to lie smoothly.

Hint: If you find your thread catching on the pins as you stitch, try pinning your pieces from behind the background fabric.

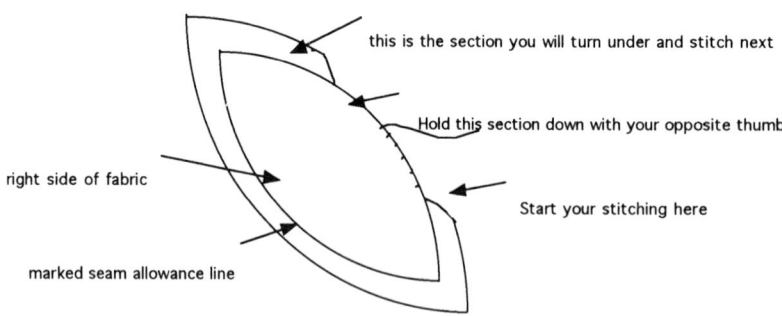

Finishing

Before you start layering the block for the quilting, take a good look at it. Is the background fabric very wrinkled? If so, you may want to smooth it out a bit before continuing. Place a fluffy, clean towel on your ironing board or some other smooth surface, and position the appliqued block with the wrong side up.

Using steam, gently go over the back of the block, just barely touching the fabric. Before it cools, smooth your hands over the fabric, helping to ease out any wrinkles. You don't want to press hard with the iron; it will flatten your applique and you will lose some of the dimension in your design.

Chapter Two: Beginning The Quilt

If there is just a little wrinkling, however, don't worry about pressing the block; that will quilt out.

Some applique techniques recommend cutting away the background fabric under the applique pieces after they have been stitched, leaving a ¼" seam allowance all around.

However, we strongly prefer leaving the background fabric in place. An applique with the backing removed will seem to collapse slightly; it loses its lovely loft and sinks into the fabric. Also, when future generations are still enjoying your quilt, if an applique should come off and the background fabric has been left intact, it is more likely to enjoy many more years of use than if a hole has been left exposed.

Again, your preference will dictate which technique you use. If you are not sure which you prefer, try both – make a sample with the background cut away, and a sample with the background left intact. See what you think!

Chapter Three

The Portable "Wrap-Around" Method

Overview

Marking Quilting

Tearing Backing Fabric

Cutting / Splicing Batting

Assembling Block for Quilting

Quilting

Joining Blocks

Preparing and Joining Borders

Overview

What is the Portable "Wrap-Around" Method?

It is a technique that makes it possible for quilters to take their quilting with them and *actually work on it* – virtually anywhere, any time. It is very difficult to carry around a quilt-in-progress, but when the work is divided into manageable segments, the work can go where you do.

With traditional quilt assembly, the top is made first, then a quilt "sandwich" is formed by layering batting between the top and the backing fabric. It is then quilted, using a hoop or frame. If you want to work on it away from home, it's almost impossible.

The wrap-around technique allows you to *complete* one block at a time, without the need for a hoop or frame. Although forming a quilt "sandwich" too, each individual block is a finished piece of work. Whether your goal is a single block for a small wallhanging, or a king-size quilt, the work is a manageable size – and you can take it with you!

Marking Quilting

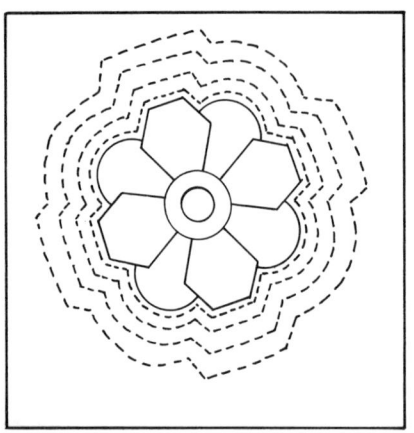

Before adding the backing and the batting, decide how you wish to quilt your block. Whatever design you decide to use, be sure to use a light hand in marking! Mark the design lightly, just dark enough to know where to place the stitching.

To make each applique piece stand out from the background and give it the most loft possible, mark your first quilting line (lightly!) around each applique piece, as close as you can without touching the applique itself. After you have completed this, mark your second quilting line, about ¼" from the first line. Each block in the book has been quilted this way.

After marking those lines, you might want to consider how you would like the background quilted. You could continue drawing lines to parallel the lines around the applique. For example, after marking the first two lines as described above, draw a third line, ⅜" from the first line, then another line, ½" from the first line, and so on, using larger spaces as you go. This is called "echo quilting," and resembles the ripples you would see on a pond after a pebble is dropped in. It is commonly seen in Hawaiian quilting, and is quite beautiful.

Another traditional background treatment is to "cross-hatch" the background, and this serves as a nice counterpoint to the flowing lines of the applique. Cross-hatching consists of parallel lines which are drawn diagonally from the corners of the block in both directions, forming a background of diamond shapes. Be sure to stop at the applique pieces, though! You don't want to stitch through the design.

You will find other background design possibilities in many books and magazines. Try whatever design appeals to you.

Chapter Three: The Portable "Wrap-Around" Method

Tearing Backing Fabric

In preparing the background fabrics, we recommend tearing the background fabrics. Tearing the fabric into the size that you need, instead of cutting, will give exact grainlines, minimize puckering and stretching, making your work easier and the finished quilt hang or lie beautifully.

To tear the fabric, first make a snip through the selvage at one end, and tear across the width of it. Snip through the selvage on the other side. Measure for the background blocks from the torn edge. Follow the cutting diagrams carefully for maximum use of your fabric, and repeat the same process for all the sections required for your project.

Cutting/Splicing Batting

Cut the batting into the size listed on your project cutting diagram. Batting that is a little larger than the size stated is no problem; it can easily be cut down if necessary. In this case, a little too big is preferable to too small.

Eventually, all quilters seem to have scraps of batting. The best way to use these small pieces is to make large pieces of them by splicing them together. This is especially helpful on the border side pieces.

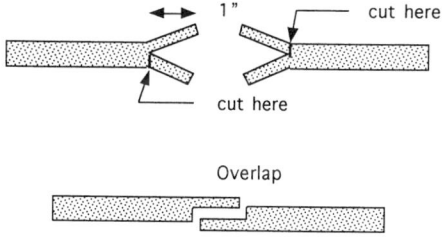

Taking two pieces of batting, determine which edges are to be spliced together. Along those edges, separate the batting into two separate layers about 1" wide. Cut off the top layer from one piece and the bottom layer from the other. Overlap these edges to make one solid piece of batting. You now have a large piece of batting that will hold up beautifully when quilted, with no telltale gap or ridge.

Assembling Block for Quilting

To layer a block, start by placing the backing fabric, wrong side up, on a flat surface. Using a ruler, mark a line 1¼" in from the edge on all four sides. Center the batting over the fabric square. (Do not trim the batting if it is too large.)

Now lay the applique block over the batting square, making sure that it is also centered. Place your hands flat in the center of the block and smooth the piece gently. Pin through all layers starting from the center, and continue smoothing and pinning as you work your way towards the edges. Pin all layers securely, with no fullness on the top or the bottom piece.

Use large round-headed pins; they are easy to handle and easy to find for removal. Check for any bubbles or pleats in the backing and the applique piece and, if necessary, readjust the pins.

Before starting to baste the block, turn the pinned square over so that the back is now facing you. Place your hands in the middle and smooth

the Rose Quilts

firmly toward the edges; you will be able to feel any fullness or wrinkles. Make any necessary adjustments.

Basting is temporary stitching which will replace the pins that are securing the block. After all the appliqueing and quilting is done, the basting threads will be removed.

To baste, use a large needle and basting thread, and securely stitch through all layers with a large basting stitch (the running stitch). Any all-purpose thread is adequate for basting purposes, but use white or a natural color, as dark colored threads will sometimes leave color behind when the basting stitches are pulled out.

Baste several lines horizontally and vertically, making a knot at the beginning of your thread and backstitching at the end of your stitching line. Do not baste around the outer edge; this will allow for any fullness in your block to be worked out as you stitch.

Quilting

Assuming you are right-handed, your left hand will be under the block as you quilt. With your left palm facing upwards, bring your thumb to meet your fingers to support the area where you will be stitching. (There will be a fold of fabric in your palm between your thumb and fingers.) This is the most effective way to hold your work without the need for a hoop.

Don't bunch up the fabric in the palm of your left hand with your thumb on top of your piece and your fingers beneath. This will almost guarantee wrinkles forming on the back of your work. You can do that when you are at the edges of the square, but while you are working on the middle section, keep your left hand completely under the block.

It's best to begin quilting in the center of the block. This allows any fullness that you did not detect to be gradually worked to the edge where it can be released.

Thread the needle with approximately 18" of quilting thread, with the end as it comes off the spool. Knot the thread with a one-loop knot where you cut it for length. This helps to minimize thread twisting and knotting that can sometimes occur. If you have trouble threading the needle this way, cut the thread at an angle.

Insert the needle in the top fabric only, about ½" from the quilting line where you wish to begin. Bring the needle out ON the quilting line, and pull gently until the knot pops through the fabric and is buried in the batting.

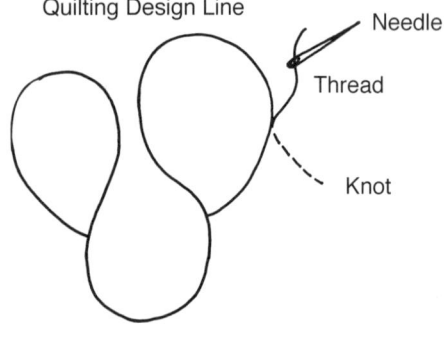

The quilting stitch is a running stitch, very similar to the basting stitch, but much, much smaller.

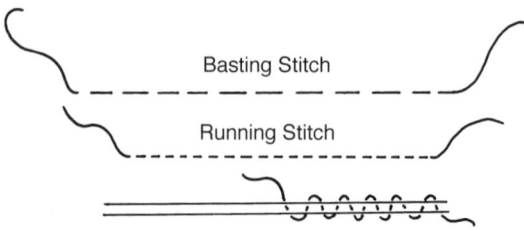

Chapter Three: The Portable "Wrap-Around" Method

At first, you may find that one stitch on the needle is all that you are comfortable with, but in time you will find that "loading the needle" with 3-5 stitches is quite manageable and speeds up the quilting considerably.

Take small, even stitches, making sure the needle goes through all layers, and pull the thread through. Beware of pulling the stitches too tight. Use just enough tension to bring the thread to rest on the surface of the block without any slackness. At first, you may find that one stitch on the needle is all that you are comfortable with, but in time you will find that "loading the needle" with 3-5 stitches is quite manageable and speeds up the quilting considerably. Although no two quilters stitch in quite the same way, try these directions as a starting point.

You will control the needle with the middle finger of your quilting hand, and in a short time it will become an automatic action. In order to control the needle in this way, you need a thimble to protect your finger.

Place the needle into the fabric vertically, then while depressing the fabric in front of the needle with your quilting hand thumb, rock the eye of the needle to your right until the needle is approximately horizontal. You can then push the needle and thread through to complete a single stitch.

If you wish to "load" with multiple stitches, before pushing the needle through, bring it back into a vertical position, then repeat the rocking action you made to form the single stitch, adding another stitch to the stitch already on your needle. Repeat this for as many stitches as you feel you can handle. You can place as many on a needle as you wish, and with just a little practice you can quilt much more quickly.

Continue quilting, following the marked lines, until there is about four inches of thread left.

To end the stitching, make a loop of the thread, put the point of the needle inside this loop and rest it at the end of the last stitch made. Do not pierce the fabric. As you pull on the thread, the loop will tighten around the needle, and slide down to the surface of the fabric, forming a small knot.

Insert the needle about one stitch length away from the knot, following your quilting pattern, into the top fabric only. Bring the needle up about ½" away from the quilting line, popping the knot through to the inside layer, just as you did at the beginning. Clip the thread at the surface of the fabric.

After stitching around the applique design, measure and mark a line 2¼" from the cut edge of the backing onto the surface of the applique block. Do not stitch your background quilting pattern past this line. When it is time to turn the backing to the front to form the sashing, this is where you will place your folded fabric edge. To make it even easier, quilt on this line all around your block. Now you have a visual placement guide, and your block is stabilized, as well.

Continue quilting until the block is finished. When you have completed two blocks, you can join them to begin the assembly of your quilt.

Joining Blocks

When you have finished quilting two blocks, you can sew them together.

Lay the two blocks back to back, lining up the edges. Pin through both backing fabrics on the line that is marked 1¼" in from the sides. Sew on this line from the top to the bottom, backstitching at each end to secure the stitches.

Open the blocks so that they are lying side by side and trim any batting that extends past the seam line. You now have two long, loose edges between the two blocks. Turn under ¼" on one of the raw edges and stitch it to the 2¼" line marked on the top of the applique block. The same stitch used for appliqueing will also work well here.

Repeat for the other block. The backing fabric has now "wrapped around" and become the sashing on the front. Following the project directions, join as many blocks as necessary to complete one row.

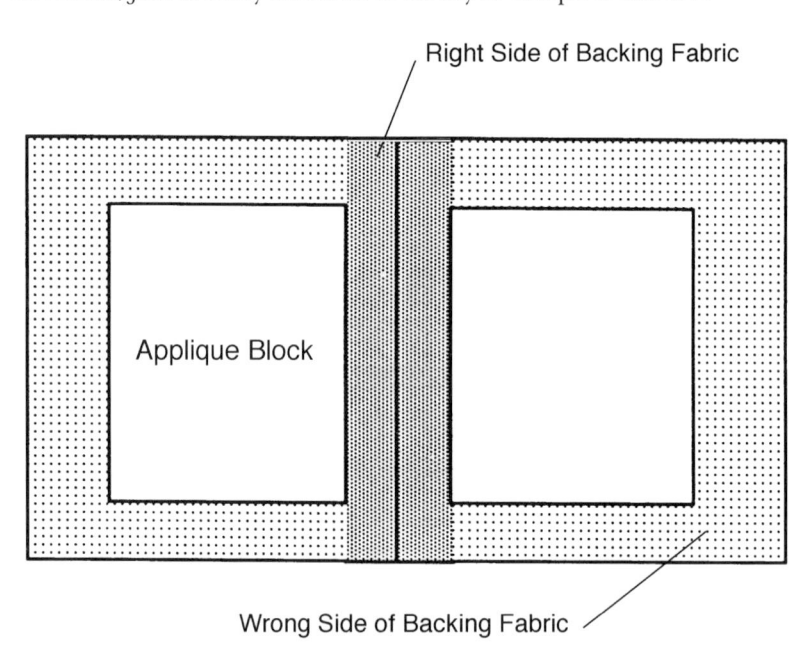

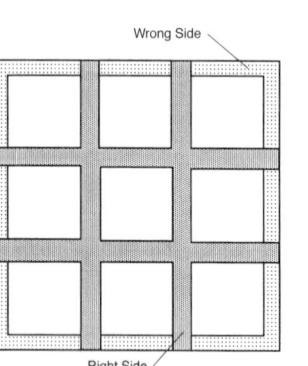

Right Side of Backing Fabric

Applique Block

Wrong Side of Backing Fabric

After you have assembled all the blocks into rows, you will then join the rows together. Starting at one end, place the first and second row back to back, just as you did with the individual blocks, and pin through the backings on the 1¼" markings, making sure that the blocks match at the seamlines. Backstitching at the beginning and the end, stitch from one end of the row to the other. Then turn under ¼" on the raw edge of each row and stitch it to the 2¼" line marked on the applique blocks.

Continue until all the rows have been assembled into one large piece, which will be your quilt without its borders.

Wrong Side

Right Side

Chapter Three: The Portable "Wrap-Around" Method

Preparing and Joining Borders

To finish your quilt, treat each border as if it were a block. When the borders are complete, sew the bottom border on first. Then sew a small block to the end of a side border, and stitch this unit to the quilt. Repeat for the other side, then add the heading at the top.

To finish the outer edges of your quilt, fold the edging on the 1¼" mark, turn under ¼" on the raw edge, and stitch into place.

Your quilt is complete. If you turn it over, you will see that it is as lovely on the back as the front. Quilting around the outside edge of the block gives it a beautifully finished look by forming a frame for the quilting within.

Now,stop, admire your beautiful work, and give yourself a pat on the back – you deserve it!

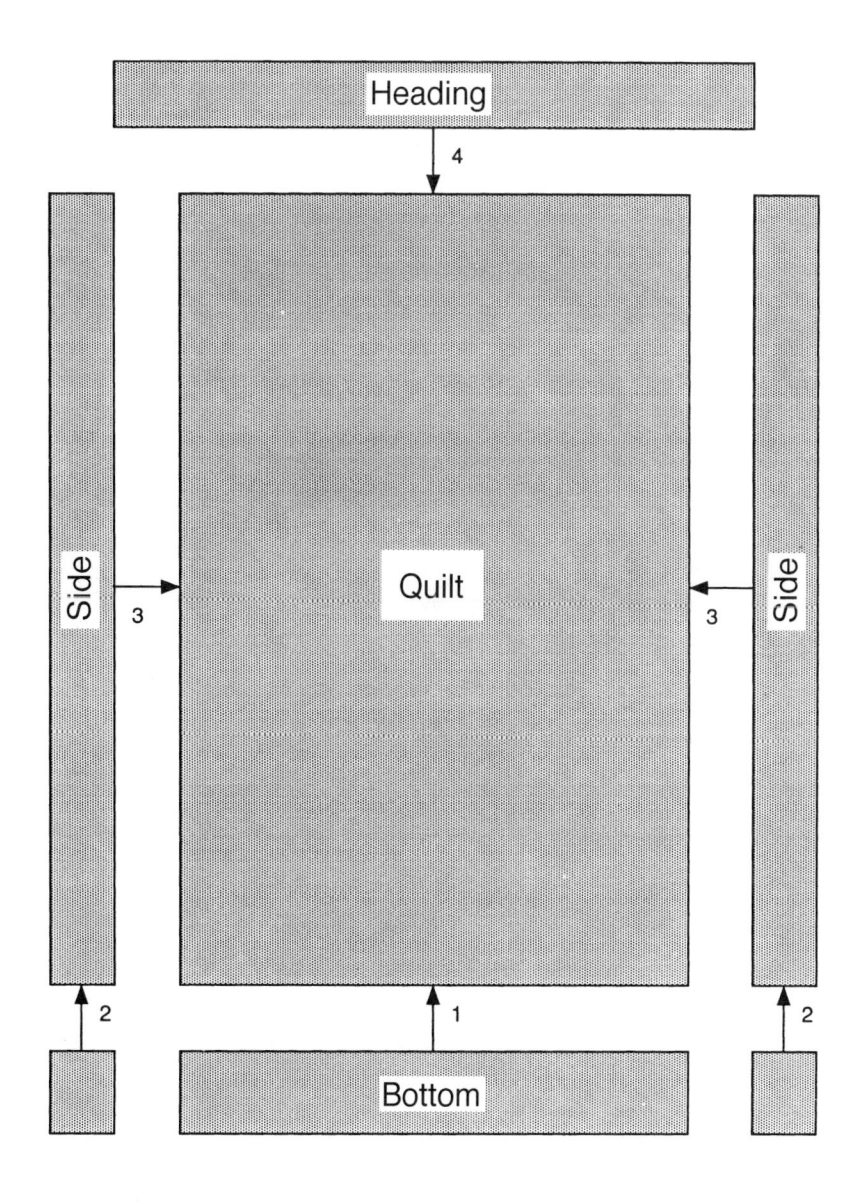

Chapter Four

Yardage Requirements and Cutting Diagrams

Wallhangings
Three-block Wallhanging

Queen-Size Quilt

King-Size Quilt

Wallhangings

Any of the blocks in this book can be made into any number of quilted items. Don't overlook the special beauty of wallhangings!

A wallhanging can be made in many configurations. Four blocks would be lovely, arranged either in straight sets or hang them "on point" (on the diagonal in a diamond shape). Three blocks joined together would fit into a narrow, long space beautifully, or could even grace a dining room as a table runner. And don't forget the possibility of hanging blocks individually, grouping them as you would paintings.

Anyway that you use them, quilts add a special warmth to a room in a way that nothing else does. Look around you and consider where you would like to enjoy your lovely work.

(See *Chapter One: Displaying Quilts*, page 17, to find out how to create a hanging "sleeve" for your quilts.)

Three-block wallhanging

Finished size 20" x 60"

Yardage requirements

Applique background fabric	1¼ yds.
Backing fabric	2 yds.
Applique designs	scraps
Batting	a crib sized batt, or batting by the yard, 1½ yds. of 48" wide batt
Cut from backing fabric	3 – 22½" squares
Cut from applique background fabric	3 – 19½" squares
Cut from the batting	3 – 20" squares

We suggest following this cutting diagram to make the most efficient use of the yardage:

BACKING FABRIC 45" 2 YDS

BACKGROUND FABRIC 45" 1 1/4 YDS

FINISHED DIMENSIONS 20" × 60"

Chapter Four: Yardage and Cutting Diagrams

Queen-Size Quilt
Finished size 84" x 100"

Yardage requirements

Applique background fabric	6 yds.
Backing fabric	9 yds.
Batting	by the yard, 6 yds. of 48" wide batting, or pre-packaged batting: 120" x 120"
Cut from backing fabric	1 strip 10½" x 86½"
	3 strips 14½" x 82½"
	12 – 22½" squares
	2 – 14½" squares
Cut from applique background fabric	1 strip 11½" x 59½"
	2 strips 11½" x 79½"
	1 strip 7½" x 83½"
	12 – 19½" squares
	2 – 11½" squares
Cut from the batting	12 – 20" squares
	2 – 12" squares
	1 strip 12" x 60"
	2 strips 12" x 80"
	1 strip 8" x 84"

We suggest following this cutting diagram to make the most efficient use of the yardage:

BACKING FABRIC 45" 9 YDS

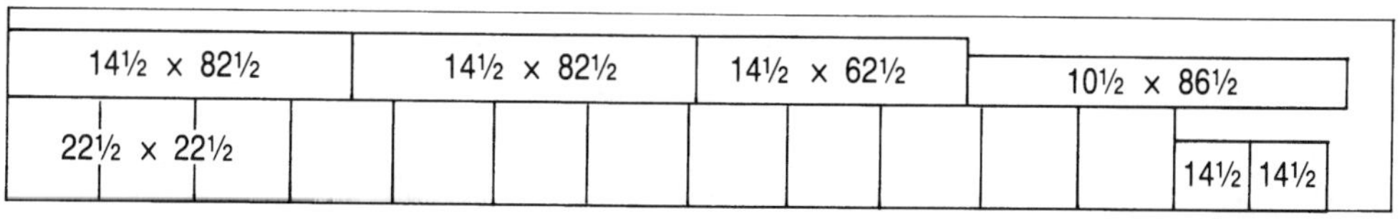

14½ x 82½ | 14½ x 82½ | 14½ x 62½ | 10½ x 86½
22½ x 22½ | | | 14½ | 14½

BACKGROUND FABRIC 45" 6 YDS

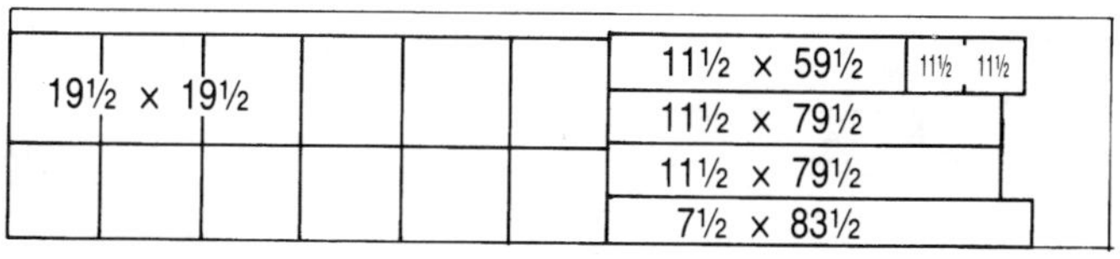

19½ x 19½ | 11½ x 59½ | 11½ | 11½
| 11½ x 79½
| 11½ x 79½
| 7½ x 83½

BATTING 48" 6 YDS

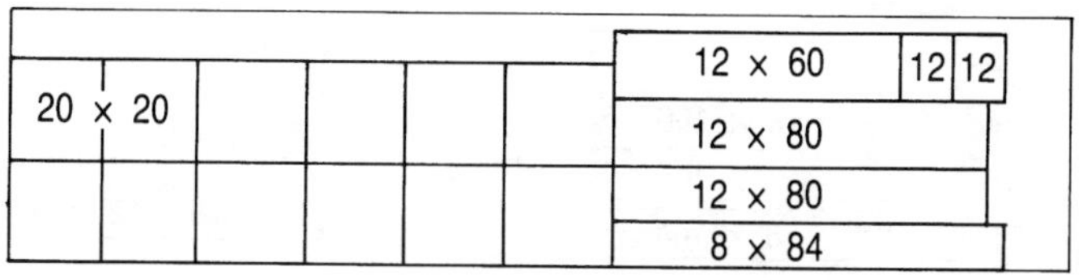

20 x 20 | 12 x 60 | 12 | 12
| 12 x 80
| 12 x 80
| 8 x 84

BATTING 120" x 120"

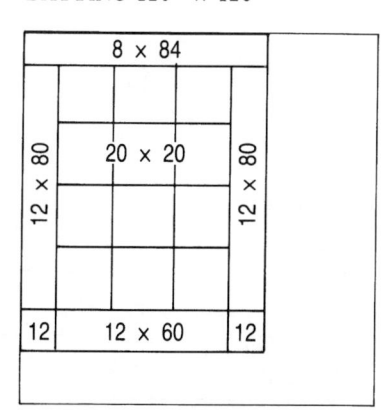

8 x 84
12 x 80 | 20 x 20 | 12 x 80
12 | 12 x 60 | 12

King-Size Quilt
Finished size 104" x 120"

Yardage requirements

Applique background fabric....................9 yds.
Backing fabric..13 yds.
Batting...by the yard,
9 yds. of 48" wide batting, or
pre-packaged batting: 120" x 120"

Cut from backing fabric..........................1 strip 10½" x 106½"
2 strips 14½" x 102½"
1 strip 14½" x 82½"
2 – 14½" squares
20 – 22½" squares

Cut from applique background fabric....1 strip 11½" x 79½"
2 strips 11½" x 99½"
1 strip 7½" x 103½"
2 – 11½" squares
20 – 19½" squares

Cut from the batting ....20 – 20" squares
2 – 12" squares
1 strip 12" x 80"
2 strips 12" x 100"
1 strip 8" x 104"

We suggest following this cutting diagram to make the most efficient use of the yardage:

BACKING FABRIC 45" 13 YDS

BACKGROUND FABRIC 45" 9 YDS

BATTING 48" 9 YDS

BATTING 120" x 120"

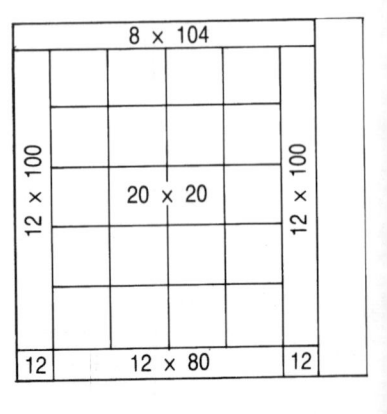

Applique and quilting: Betty Cossey   Photography: Jon Anderson

*T*his colorful quilt, *Rose Sampler II*, shows bold use of color and contrast. Each of the 12 blocks is a different rose applique pattern, yet harmony and balance is achieved by repeating the same fabrics throughout. The sashing between the blocks is created from the backing fabric, and is brought to the front during the "wrap-around" step.

	A			
	1	2	3	
	4	5	6	
B	7	8	9	B
	10	11	12	
C		B		C

(1) *Rambling Rose*
(2) *Oregon Rose*
(3) *Topeka Rose*
(4) *Country Rose*
(5) *Harrison Rose*
(6) *Rose and Tulip*
(7) *Heartfelt Rose*
(8) *Wild Rose*
(9) *Circle of Roses*
(10) *Indiana Rose*
(11) *Ohio Rose*
(12) *Rose Wreath*
(A) *Rose Sampler Heading*
(B) *Rose Sampler Border*
(C) *Rose Sampler Corner*

Applique and quilting: Barbara Webb   Photography: Jon Anderson

Shown here is a delightful, almost-finished quilt, displayed in Nancy Eder's colorful *Country Lady Quilt Shop* in Roseburg, Oregon.

The lower central block is the *Rose and Tulip* applique pattern, and the block above gives a glimpse of the *Ohio Rose* pattern.

These two brown teddies (who live happily at Tolly's "Beckley House" Bed and Breakfast), are snug and warm under their one-block *Country Rose* pattern quilt.

Applique and quilting: Betty Cossey   Photography: Jon Anderson

These blocks add a fresh, quilted charm to a country dining room table.

Top – Country Rose
Middle – Rose of Sharon
Bottom – Rose Wreath

Applique and quilting: Betty Cossey   Photography: Jon Anderson

These two bright blocks illustrate the look of a work-in-progress. The top block (*Whig Rose* applique pattern) has been joined to the bottom block (*Rambling Rose* applique pattern) using the wrap-around method, forming the sashing between the blocks. The outer edges remain unfinished, waiting to be sewn to other blocks, or turned and finished for a pretty, two-block wallhanging.

Top – Whig Rose
Bottom – Rambling Rose
Sashing – formed by the wrap-around method

Applique and quilting: Betty Cossey   Photography: Jon Anderson

The simple beauty of this one-block wallhanging is the perfect example that your wrap-around quilting project doesn't have to be complicated or time-consuming! The *Rose of Sharon* applique pattern adds just the right amount of interest and color to this doll's quiet corner.

Applique and quilting: Betty Cossey   Photography: Jon Anderson

Applique and quilting: Betty Cossey   Photography: Jon Anderson

A *Topeka Rose* applique design graces this simple, charming quilt made with soft pinks, reds and greens, and the floral backing becomes the sashing.

The softly hued *Topeka Rose Quilt* is the focal point of this simple cozy bedroom.

A – no applique on this quilted block
B – *Topeka Rose* applique pattern
1 – hand-quilting only on the heading and corner blocks
2 – the borders are created from elements of the *Topeka Rose* applique design connected with a curving "vine" made from bias strips.

*T*he *Old Rose Quilt* complements the atmosphere of a by-gone era in the charming Garden Suite bedroom of Tolly's "Beckley House" Bed and Breakfast. (See the next page for the names of the applique patterns.)

A delicate tracery of vines, roses and buds surrounds the two applique patterns repeated in this quilt of old-world charm. The *Old Rose Quilt* uses the same fabric for the applique block background, the border and corner background, and the backing fabric. This creates a "seamless" look when using the portable, wrap-around method to join the finished blocks.

Applique and quilting: Betty Cossey   Original Design: Pat Andreatta   Design Variation: Betty Cossey   Photography: Jon Anderson

A – *Bud and Rose Wreath (Variation)*
B – *Patriot's Rose (Variation)*
1 – *Old Rose Heading*
2 – *Old Rose Border*
3 – *Old Rose Corner*

	1			
	A	B	A	
	B	A	B	
2	A	B	A	2
	B	A	B	
3	2			3

Applique and quilting: Betty Cossey   Photography: Jon Anderson

T his lovely quilt, *Rose Sampler I* (shown on our cover), has 12 blocks, each a different applique pattern. While each block has its own distinctive flair, the use of the same fabrics throughout the quilt provides a unifying harmony.

	A		
	1	2	3
B	4	5	6	B
	7	8	9
	10	11	12
C		B		C

(1) *Indiana Rose*
(2) *Circle of Roses*
(3) *Topeka Rose*
(4) *Rose and Tulip*
(5) *Wild Rose*
(6) *Rose of Sharon*
(7) *Rose Wreath*
(8) *Harrison Rose*
(9) *Rose and Coxcomb*
(10) *Ohio Rose*
(11) *Oregon Rose*
(12) *Country Rose*
(A) *Rose Sampler Heading*
(B) *Rose Sampling Border*
(C) *Rose Sampler Corner*

Chapter Five

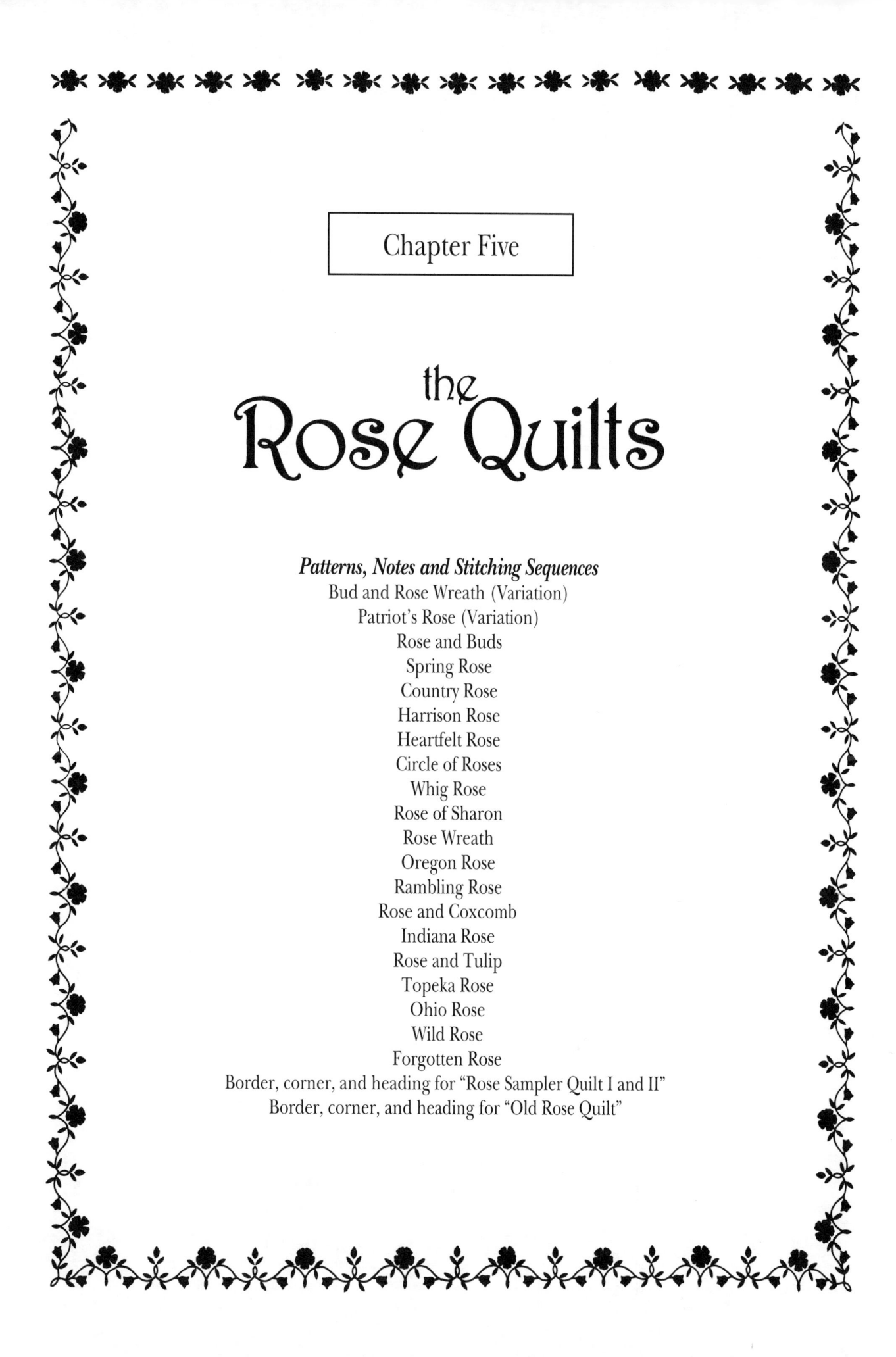

the Rose Quilts

Patterns, Notes and Stitching Sequences
Bud and Rose Wreath (Variation)
Patriot's Rose (Variation)
Rose and Buds
Spring Rose
Country Rose
Harrison Rose
Heartfelt Rose
Circle of Roses
Whig Rose
Rose of Sharon
Rose Wreath
Oregon Rose
Rambling Rose
Rose and Coxcomb
Indiana Rose
Rose and Tulip
Topeka Rose
Ohio Rose
Wild Rose
Forgotten Rose
Border, corner, and heading for "Rose Sampler Quilt I and II"
Border, corner, and heading for "Old Rose Quilt"

the Rose Quilts

Pattern Table

	Bud and Rose Wreath (Variation)	Patriot's Rose (Variation)	Rose and Buds
Spring Rose	Country Rose	Harrison Rose	Heartfelt Rose
Circle of Roses	Whig Rose	Rose of Sharon	Rose Wreath
Oregon Rose	Rambling Rose	Rose and Coxcomb	Indiana Rose
Rose and Tulip	Topeka Rose	Ohio Rose	Wild Rose
Forgotten Rose		◁ Rose Sampler I and II Border, Corner and Heading	
		Old Rose Quilt Border, Corner and Heading ▷	

Chapter Five: the Rose Quilts

Bud and Rose Wreath (Variation)

Original design: Pat Andreatta
Variation: Betty Cossey

This is one of the two patterns shown on the king-sized quilt, *Old Rose Quilt*.
Stitch the design in this sequence: stems – S-1, S-2, S-3, S-4
leaves – L-1, L-2, L-3
buds – B-1, B-2, B-3
flower – F-1, F-2

Bud and Rose Wreath (Variation)

Trace this pattern four times and join together to form complete design. See page 20, *Tracing Patterns*, for complete instructions. NOTE: As all patterns are hand-drawn, some adjustment may be necessary for pattern lines to meet.

Chapter Five: the Rose Quilts

Patriot's Rose (Variation)

Original design: Pat Andreatta
Variation: Betty Cossey

This is one of the two patterns shown on the king-sized quilt, *Old Rose Quilt*.
Stitch the design in this sequence: stems – S-1, S-2
leaves – L
tulip – T
bud – B-1, B-2, B-3, B-4
flower – F-1, F-2, F-3

Patriot's Rose (Variation)

Trace this pattern four times and join together to form complete design. See page 20, *Tracing Patterns*, for complete instructions. NOTE: As all patterns are hand-drawn, some adjustment may be necessary for pattern lines to meet.

Chapter Five: the Rose Quilts

Rose and Buds

Stitch this design in the following sequence: bud – B-1, B-2
stem – S
leaves – L
center flower – C-1, C-2*, C-3, C-4*, C-5
*C-2 is a circle with C-3 appliqued on top
*C-4 is a circle with C-5 appliqued on top

Rose and Buds

Trace this pattern four times and join together to form complete design. See page 20, *Tracing Patterns*, for complete instructions. NOTE: As all patterns are hand-drawn, some adjustment may be necessary for pattern lines to meet.

Chapter Five: the Rose Quilts

Spring Rose

Stitch this design in the following sequence: leaf – L-1*
stem – S
leaf – L-2*
petals – P-1, P-2, P-3, P-4, P-5
bud – B-1, B-2, B-3

*leaf L-1 is under the stem and must be stitched first; after the stem is stitched, then L-2 is stitched

Spring Rose

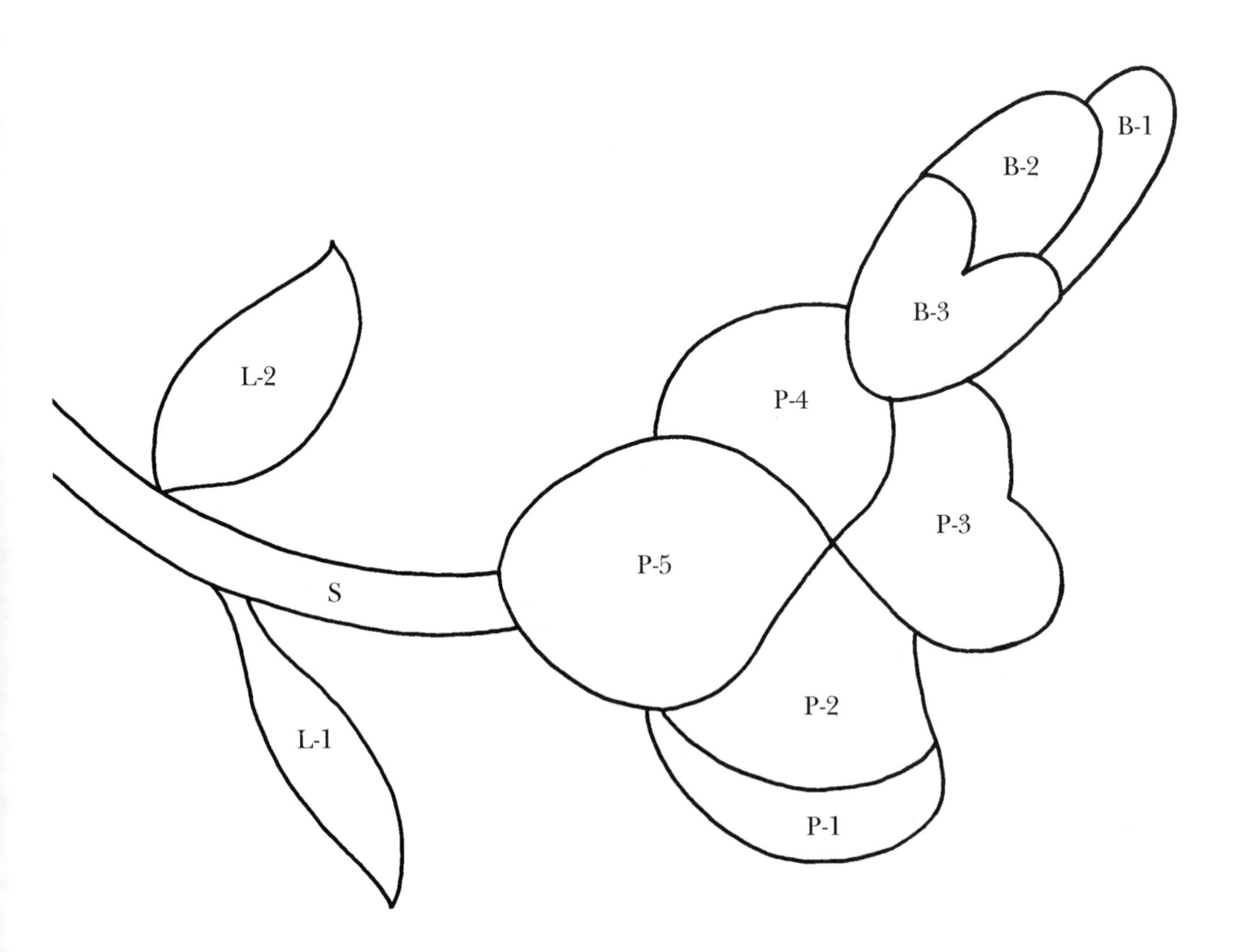

Trace this pattern four times and join together to form complete design. See page 20, *Tracing Patterns*, for complete instructions. NOTE: As all patterns are hand-drawn, some adjustment may be necessary for pattern lines to meet.

Chapter Five: the Rose Quilts

Country Rose

Stitch this design in the following sequence: leaves – L
　　　　　　　　　　　　　　　　　　　stem – S
　　　　　　　　　　　　　　　　　　　bud – B-1, B-2, B-3
　　　　　　　　　　　　　　　　　　　flower – F-1, F-2, F-3

Country Rose

F-3
F-2
F-1
L
S
L
B-2
B-3
B-1

Trace this pattern four times and join together to form complete design. See page 20, *Tracing Patterns*, for complete instructions. NOTE: As all patterns are hand-drawn, some adjustment may be necessary for pattern lines to meet.

the Rose Quilts

Chapter Five: the Rose Quilts

Harrison Rose

Stitch this design in the following sequence: stem – S
                                             leaves – L
                                             flower – F-1, F-2
                                             center flower – C-1, C-2, C-3*, C-4
                                             *C-3 is a circle with C-4 appliqued on top

Harrison Rose

Trace this pattern four times and join together to form complete design. See page 20, *Tracing Patterns*, for complete instructions. NOTE: As all patterns are hand-drawn, some adjustment may be necessary for pattern lines to meet.

Chapter Five: the Rose Quilts

Heartfelt Rose

Stitch this design in the following sequence: stem – S-1, S-2
leaves – L-1, L-2 (applies to both the large and small leaves)
flower – F-1, F-2, F-3

Heartfelt Rose

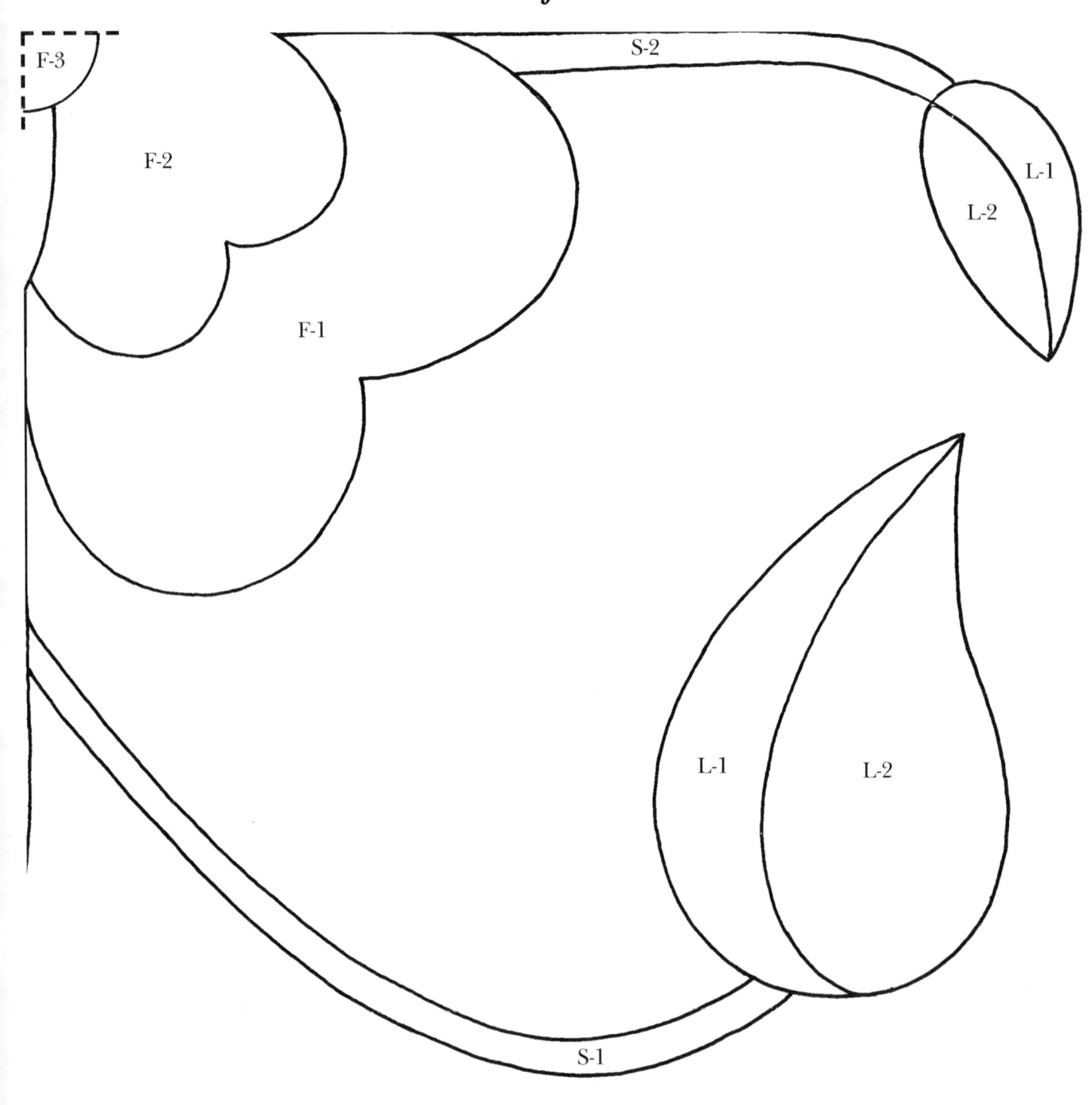

Trace this pattern four times and join together to form complete design. See page 20, *Tracing Patterns*, for complete instructions. NOTE: As all patterns are hand-drawn, some adjustment may be necessary for pattern lines to meet.

Chapter Five: the Rose Quilts

Circle of Roses

Stitch this design in the following sequence: stem – S
                                                        leaves – L
                                                        flower – F-1, F-2
                                                        center flower – C-1, C-2, C-3

68

the Rose Quilts

Circle of Roses

C-3
C-2
C-1
L
L
S
L
F-1
F-2

Trace this pattern four times and join together to form complete design. See page 20, *Tracing Patterns*, for complete instructions. NOTE: As all patterns are hand-drawn, some adjustment may be necessary for pattern lines to meet.

Chapter Five: the Rose Quilts

Whig Rose

Stitch this design in the following sequence: stems – S
leaves – L
bud – B-1, B-2, B-3
flower – F-1, F-2, F-3

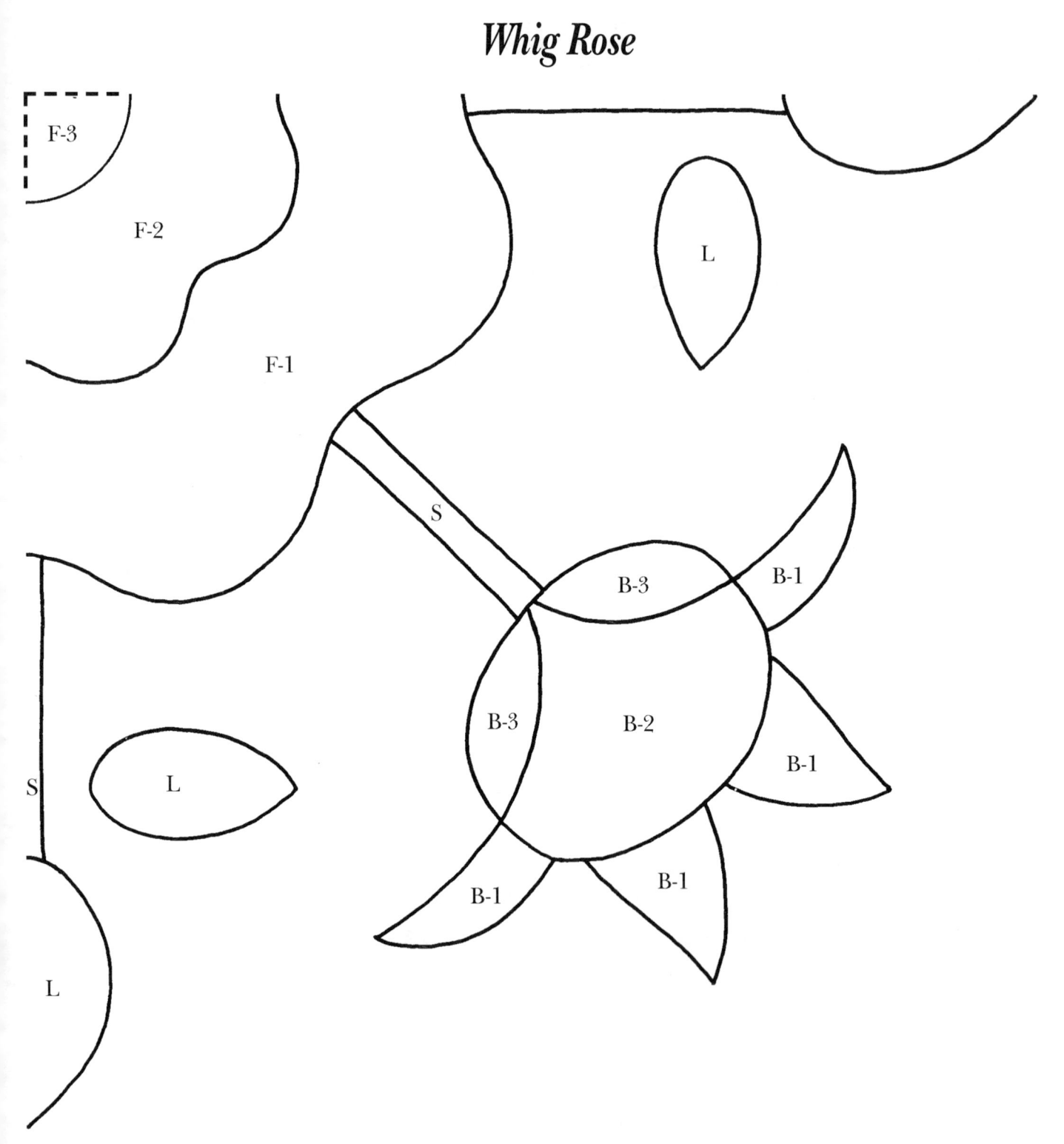

Whig Rose

Trace this pattern four times and join together to form complete design. See page 20, *Tracing Patterns*, for complete instructions. NOTE: As all patterns are hand-drawn, some adjustment may be necessary for pattern lines to meet.

Chapter Five: the Rose Quilts

Rose of Sharon

Stitch this design in the following sequence: stems – S-1, S-2
leaves – L
buds – B-1, B-2
large leaf – H-1, H-2
flower – F-1, F-2*, F-3
*F-2 is a circle with F-3 appliqued on top

Rose of Sharon

Trace this pattern four times and join together to form complete design. See page 20, *Tracing Patterns*, for complete instructions. NOTE: As all patterns are hand-drawn, some adjustment may be necessary for pattern lines to meet.

Chapter Five: the Rose Quilts

Rose Wreath

Stitch this design in the following sequence: leaves – L
bud – B-1, B-2, B-3
stem – S
flower – F-1, F-2, F-3

Rose Wreath

Trace this pattern four times and join together to form complete design. See page 20, *Tracing Patterns*, for complete instructions. NOTE: As all patterns are hand-drawn, some adjustment may be necessary for pattern lines to meet.

Chapter Five: the Rose Quilts

Oregon Rose

Stitch this design in the following sequence: leaves – L
stems – S-1, S-2
buds – B-1, B-2, B-3 (applies to both the large and small bud)
flower – F-1, F-2, F-3

the Rose Quilts

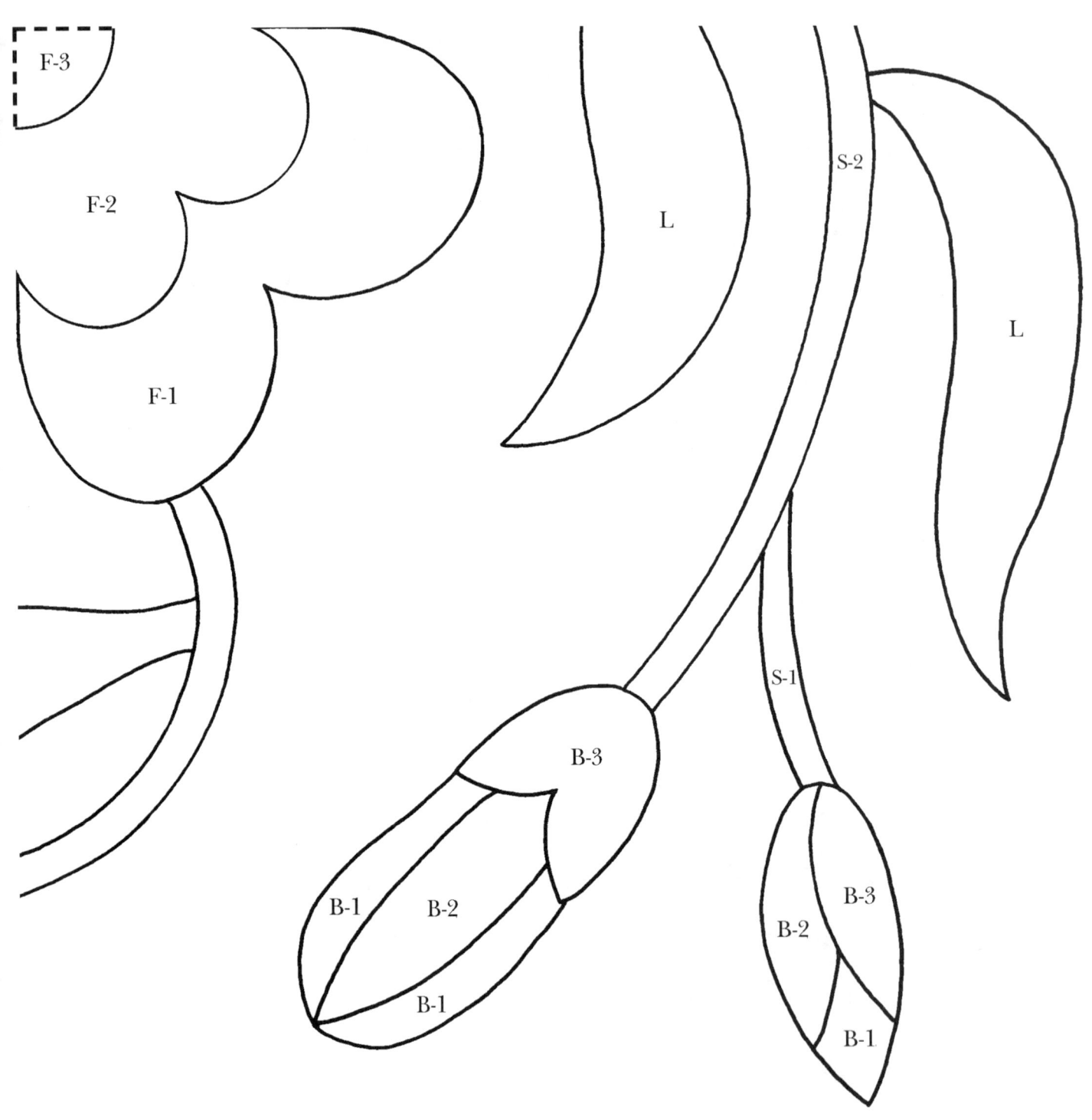

Oregon Rose

Trace this pattern four times and join together to form complete design. See page 20, *Tracing Patterns*, for complete instructions. NOTE: As all patterns are hand-drawn, some adjustment may be necessary for pattern lines to meet.

Chapter Five: the Rose Quilts

Rambling Rose

Stitch this design in the following sequence: leaves – L
stem – S
bud – B-1, B-2
flower – F-1, F-2, F-3

78 the Rose Quilts

Rambling Rose

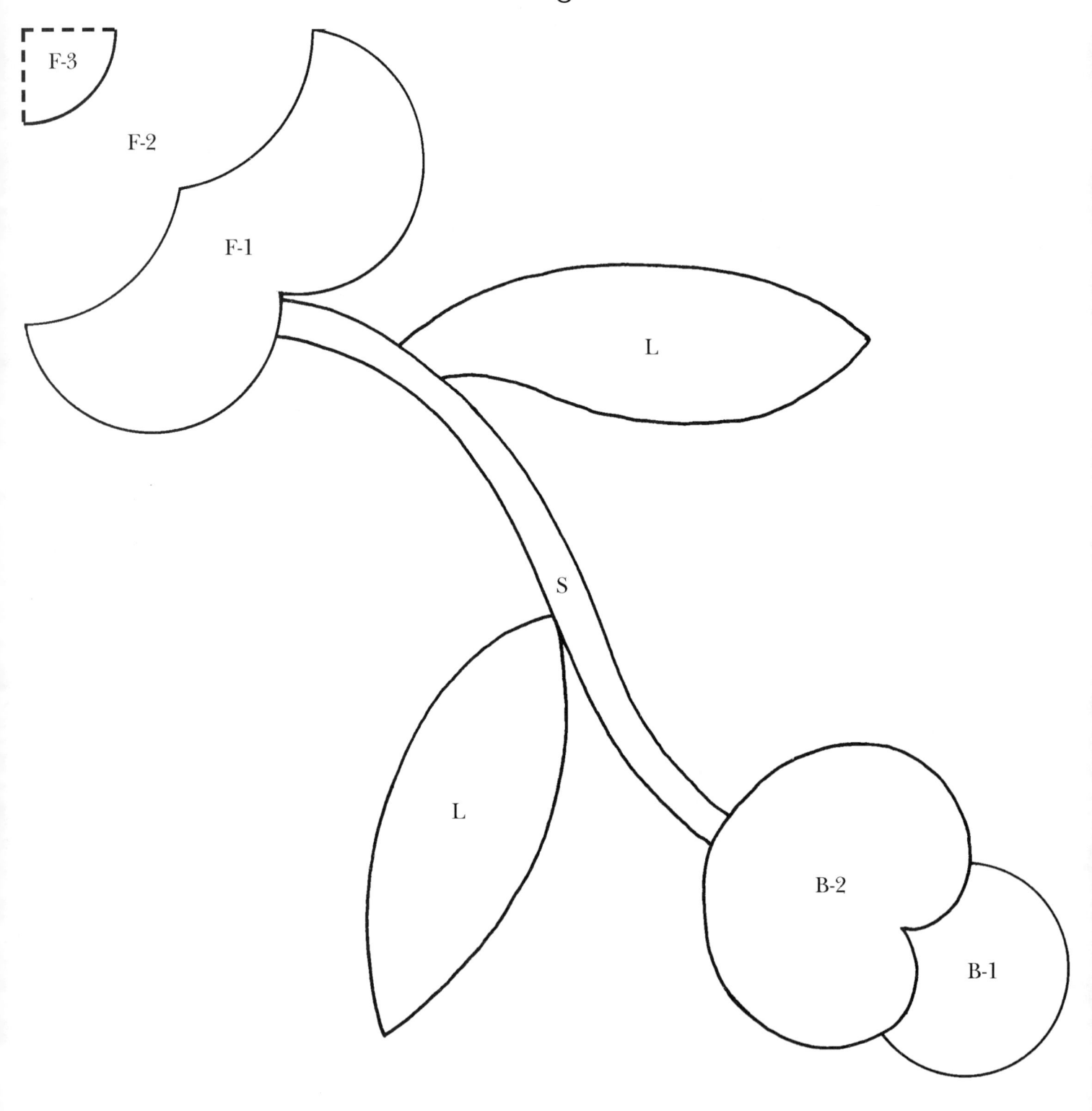

F-3

F-2

F-1

L

S

L

B-2

B-1

Trace this pattern four times and join together to form complete design. See page 20, *Tracing Patterns*, for complete instructions. NOTE: As all patterns are hand-drawn, some adjustment may be necessary for pattern lines to meet.

Chapter Five: the Rose Quilts

Rose and Coxcomb

Stitch this design in the following sequence: stem – S
leaves – L
bud – B-1, B-2, B-3
flower – F-1, F-2

Rose and Coxcomb

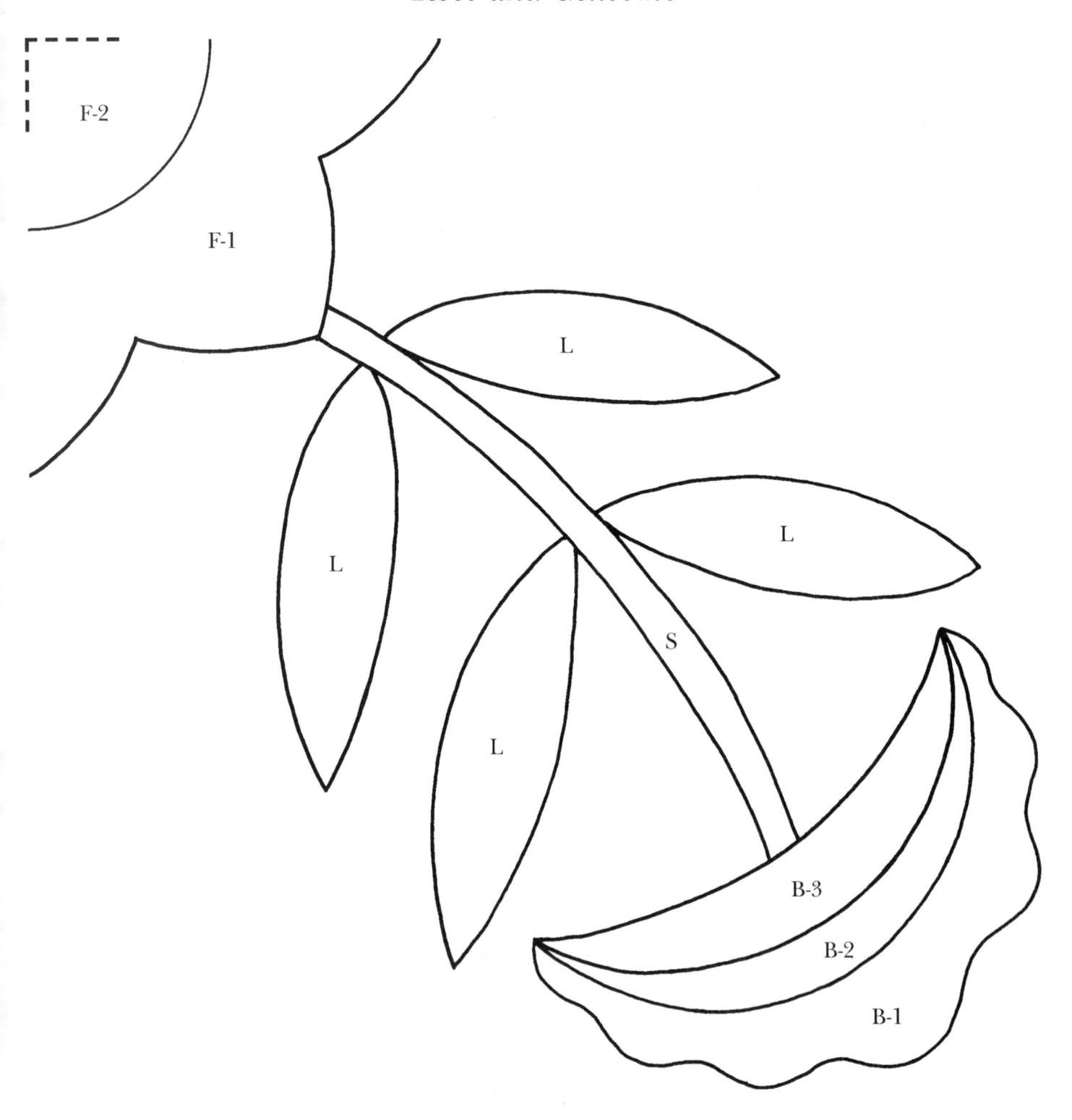

F-2

F-1

L

L

L

L

S

B-3

B-2

B-1

the Rose Quilts

Trace this pattern four times and join together to form complete design. See page 20, *Tracing Patterns*, for complete instructions. NOTE: As all patterns are hand-drawn, some adjustment may be necessary for pattern lines to meet.

Chapter Five: the Rose Quilts

Indiana Rose

Stitch this design in the following sequence: leaves – L
                                                                                   bud – B-1, B-2
                                                                                   stem – S
                                                                                   flower – F-1, F-2

Indiana Rose

F-2
F-1
L
L
L
L
S
B-2
B-1

Trace this pattern four times and join together to form complete design. See page 20, *Tracing Patterns*, for complete instructions. NOTE: As all patterns are hand-drawn, some adjustment may be necessary for pattern lines to meet.

Chapter Five: the Rose Quilts

Rose and Tulip

Stitch this design in the following sequence: leaves – L-1
stem – S
leaves – L-2
tulip – T
flower – F-1, F-2

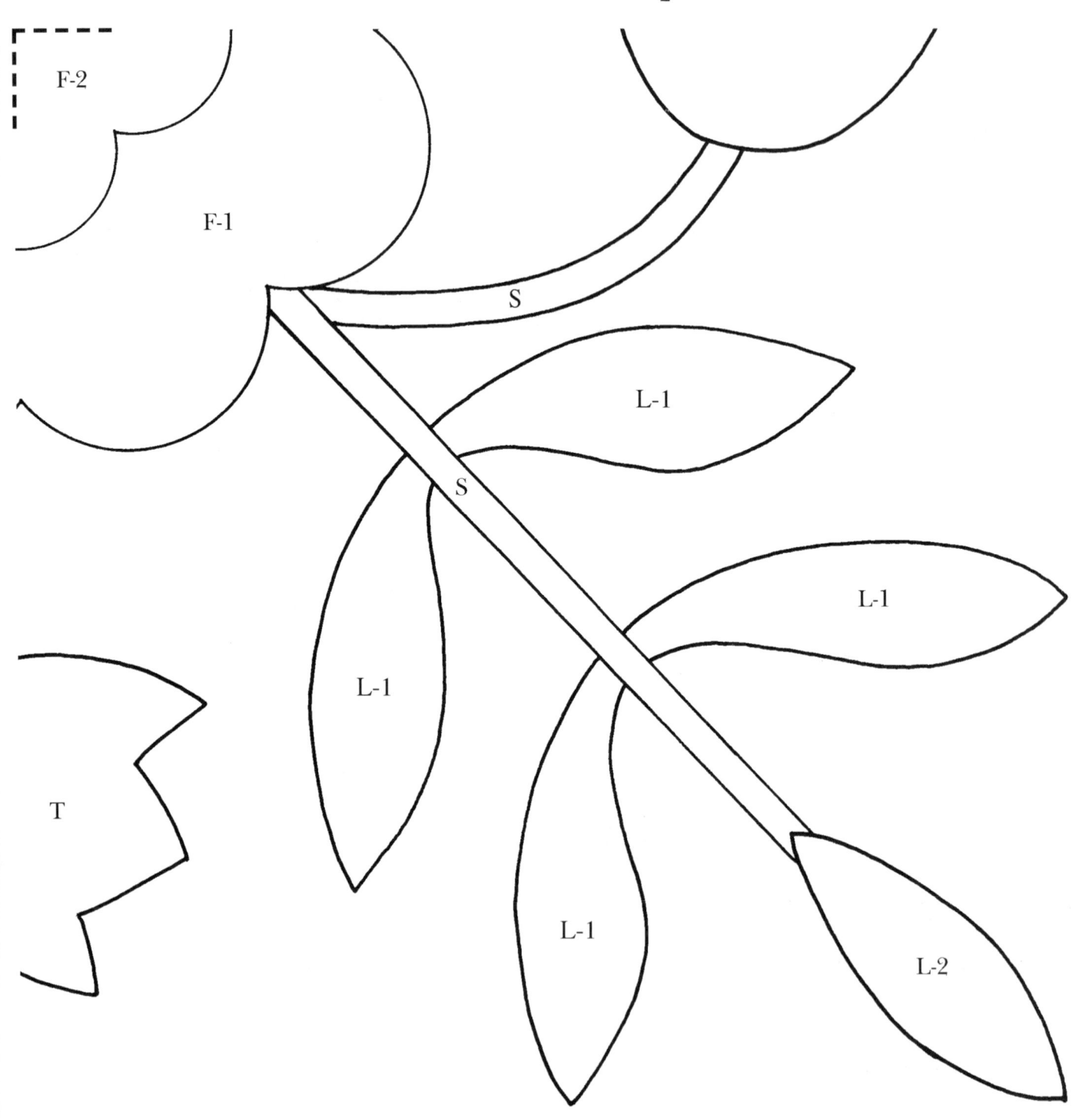

Rose and Tulip

Trace this pattern four times and join together to form complete design. See page 20, *Tracing Patterns*, for complete instructions. NOTE: As all patterns are hand-drawn, some adjustment may be necessary for pattern lines to meet.

Chapter Five: the Rose Quilts

Topeka Rose

Stitch this design in the following sequence: leaves – L
stem – S
bud – B-1, B-2
flower – F-1, F-2, F-3

86

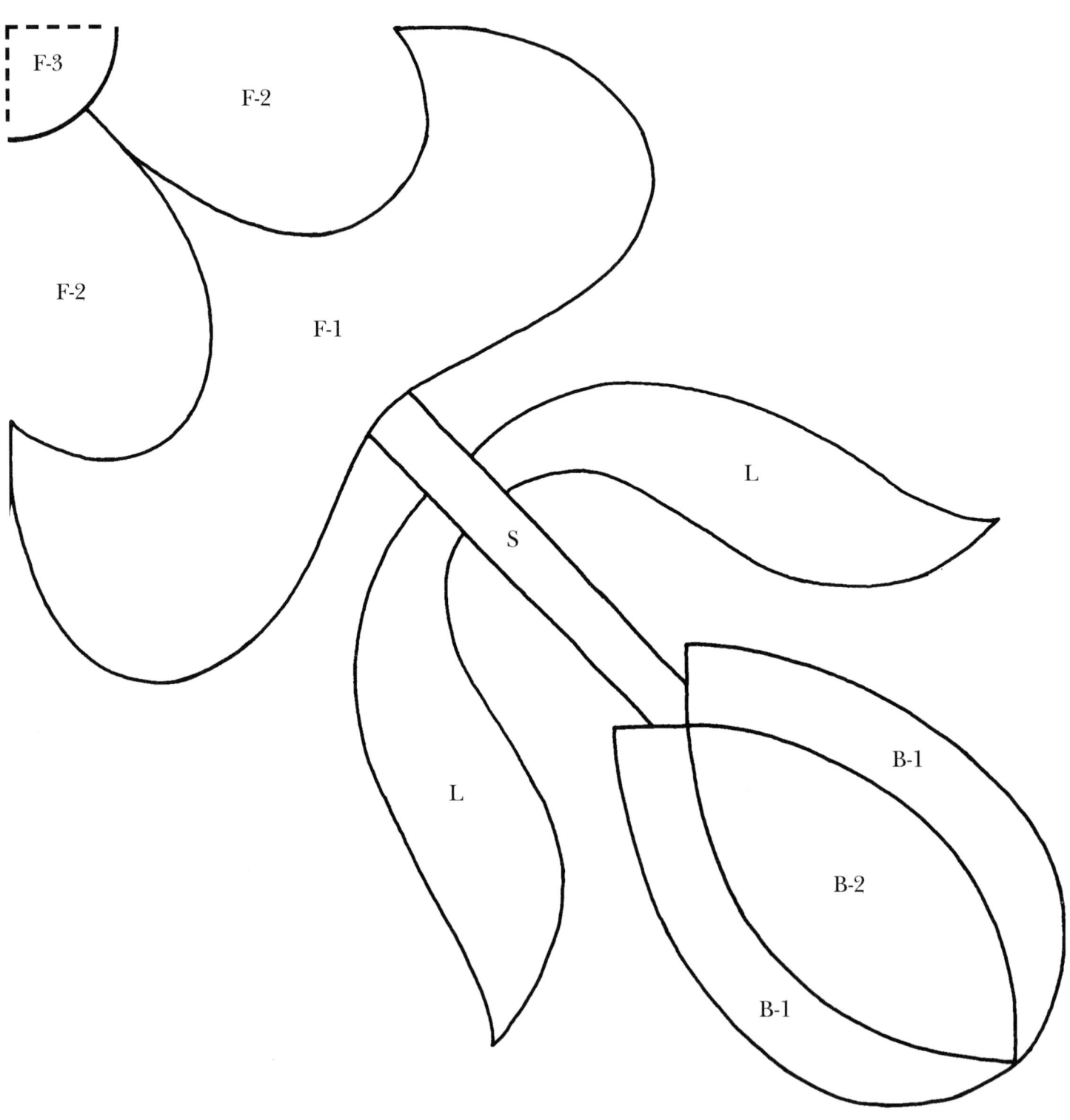

the Rose Quilts

Topeka Rose

F-3
F-2
F-2
F-1
L
S
L
B-1
B-2
B-1

Trace this pattern four times and join together to form complete design. See page 20, *Tracing Patterns*, for complete instructions. NOTE: As all patterns are hand-drawn, some adjustment may be necessary for pattern lines to meet.

Chapter Five: the Rose Quilts

Ohio Rose

Stitch this design in the following sequence: bud – B-1, B-2
flower – F-1, F-2, F-3

Ohio Rose

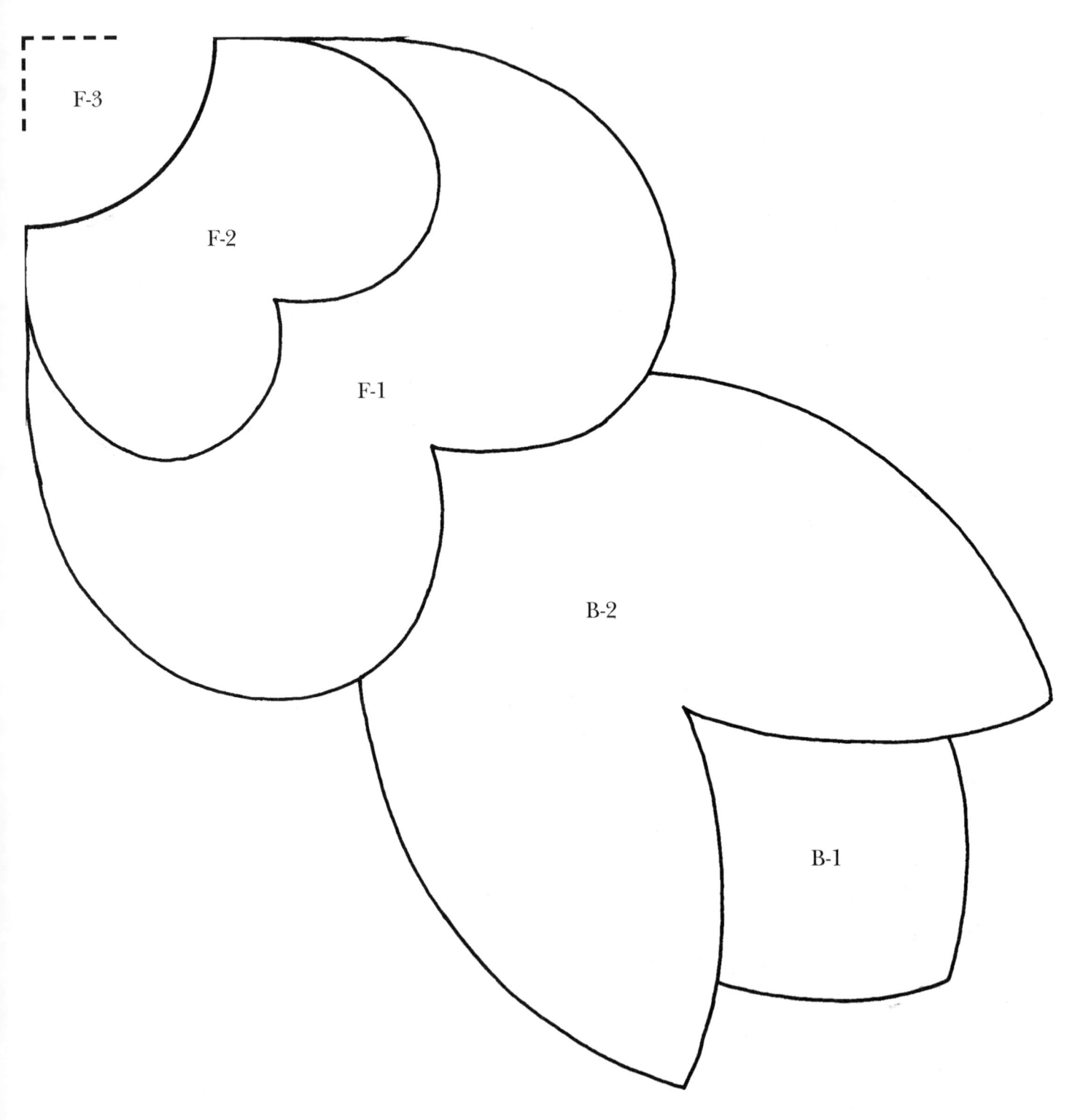

F-3

F-2

F-1

B-2

B-1

Trace this pattern four times and join together to form complete design. See page 20, *Tracing Patterns*, for complete instructions. NOTE: As all patterns are hand-drawn, some adjustment may be necessary for pattern lines to meet.

Chapter Five: the Rose Quilts

Wild Rose

Stitch this design in the following sequence: stem – S
　　　　　　　　　　　　　　　　　　　　leaves – L
　　　　　　　　　　　　　　　　　　　　bud – B-1, B-2, B-3
　　　　　　　　　　　　　　　　　　　　flower – F-1, F-2, F-3

Wild Rose

Trace this pattern four times and join together to form complete design. See page 20, *Tracing Patterns*, for complete instructions. NOTE: As all patterns are hand-drawn, some adjustment may be necessary for pattern lines to meet.

Chapter Five: the Rose Quilts

Forgotten Rose

Stitch this design in the following sequence: leaves – L
flower – F-1, F-2, F-3, F-4

Forgotten Rose

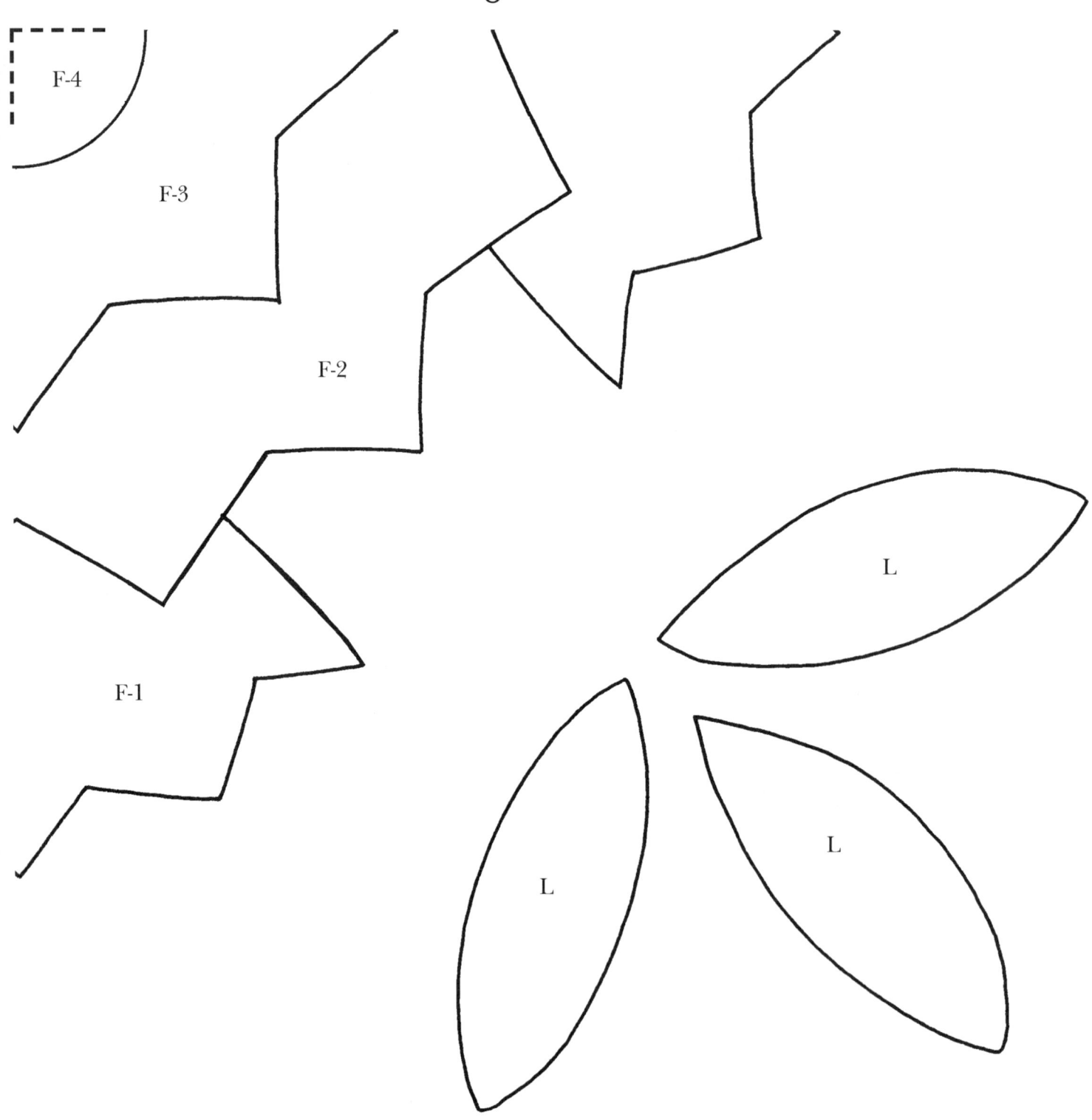

F-4

F-3

F-2

F-1

L

L

L

Trace this pattern four times and join together to form complete design. See page 20, *Tracing Patterns*, for complete instructions. NOTE: As all patterns are hand-drawn, some adjustment may be necessary for pattern lines to meet.

the Rose Quilts

Chapter Five: the Rose Quilts

Rose Sampler I and II – Border, Corners, and Heading

Corner Flower

Heading Flower

Border

Rose Sampler I and II – Corner Flower

Trace this pattern twice (for bottom left and right corners).

NOTE: As all patterns are hand-drawn, some adjustment may be necessary for pattern lines to meet.

Chapter Five: the Rose Quilts

Rose Sampler I and II – Heading Flower

Trace this entire pattern five times: trace flower portion only four times and join as shown on pages 43 and 50.

NOTE: As all patterns are hand-drawn, some adjustment may be necessary for pattern lines to meet.

Rose Sampler I and II – Border (left segment)

Trace this pattern 11 times (once for each repeat of border pattern). Join as shown on pages 43 and 50.

NOTE: As all patterns are hand-drawn, some adjustment may be necessary for pattern lines to meet.

Chapter Five: the Rose Quilts

Rose Sampler I and II – Border (center segment)

Trace this pattern 11 times (once for each repeat of border pattern). Join as shown on pages 43 and 50.

NOTE: As all patterns are hand-drawn, some adjustment may be necessary for pattern lines to meet.

Rose Sampler I and II – Border (right segment)

the Rose Quilts

Trace this pattern 11 times (once for each repeat of border pattern). Join as shown on pages 43 and 50.

NOTE: As all patterns are hand-drawn, some adjustment may be necessary for pattern lines to meet.

Chapter Five: the Rose Quilts

Old Rose Quilt – Border, Corners, and Heading

Border

Heading Flower

Corner Vine

Old Rose Quilt – Heading Flower

Trace this pattern seven times and join as shown on page 49.

NOTE: As all patterns are hand-drawn, some adjustment may be necessary for pattern lines to meet.

Chapter Five: the Rose Quilts

Old Rose Quilt – Border Vine (left segment)

Trace this pattern eight times (once for each repeat of border pattern). Join as shown on page 49.

NOTE: As all patterns are hand-drawn, some adjustment may be necessary for pattern lines to meet.

Old Rose Quilt – Border Vine *(center segment)*

Trace this pattern 11 times (once for each repeat of border pattern). Join as shown on page 49.

NOTE: As all patterns are hand-drawn, some adjustment may be necessary for pattern lines to meet.

Chapter Five: the Rose Quilts

Old Rose Quilt – Border Vine (right segment)

Trace this pattern 11 times (once for each repeat of border pattern). Join as shown on page 49.

NOTE: As all patterns are hand-drawn, some adjustment may be necessary for pattern lines to meet.

Old Rose Quilt – Corner Vine (left segment)

Trace this pattern twice (once for each corner). Join as shown on page 49.

NOTE: As all patterns are hand-drawn, some adjustment may be necessary for pattern lines to meet.

Chapter Five: the Rose Quilts

Old Rose Quilt – Corner Vine (corner segment)

Trace this pattern twice (once for each corner). Join as shown on page 49.

NOTE: As all patterns are hand-drawn, some adjustment may be necessary for pattern lines to meet.

Old Rose Quilt – Corner Vine (upper segment)

Note: Turn this pattern piece sideways to match lines on corner vine (corner segment)

Trace this pattern twice (once for each corner). Join as shown on page 49.

NOTE: As all patterns are hand-drawn, some adjustment may be necessary for pattern lines to meet.

Chapter Five: the Rose Quilts

107

Pattern Table

	Bud and Rose Wreath (Variation)	Patriot's Rose (Variation)	Rose and Buds
Spring Rose	Country Rose	Harrison Rose	Heartfelt Rose
Circle of Roses	Whig Rose	Rose of Sharon	Rose Wreath
Oregon Rose	Rambling Rose	Rose and Coxcomb	Indiana Rose
Rose and Tulip	Topeka Rose	Ohio Rose	Wild Rose
Forgotten Rose		◁ Rose Sampler I and II Border, Corner and Heading	
		Old Rose Quilt Border, Corner and Heading ▷	

Mail Order Sources

For any of the quilting and sewing notions mentioned in this book, we recommend that you first check with your local quilt or fabric store. If you have difficulty locating any items, we recommend the following mail order sources.

Pat Andreatta is the author of several excellent applique books and patterns, and has designed a variety of notions for use with applique. For a full list of titles, as well as a description of quilting items, check with your local quilt shop or write to Pat Andreatta, Heirloom Stitches, 626 Shadowood Lane, Warren, OH 44484.

Clotilde's catalog supplies a variety of sewing and quilting items. Call their order line at 800-772-2891, or write Clotilde, 1909 S.W. First Ave., Ft. Lauderdale, FL 33315-2100.

Philomena Durcan has developed metal bias press bars that you can order directly by writing to 834 W. Remington, Sunnyvale, CA 94087, or call her at 408-735-8049.

Keepsake Quilting offers a catalog of quilting supplies, books and notions. Call them at 603-253-8731, or write Keepsake Quilting, Route 25, P. O. Box 1618, Centre Harbor, NH 03226-1618 for your copy.

Nancy's Notions presents a catalog full of sewing and quilting goodies. Call them at 800-833-0690 for your free copy, or write Nancy's Notions, P. O. Box 683, Beaver Dam, WI 53916-9976.

Product Information

Disappearing Ink Marking Pen is made by Dritz Corporation.

Mark-B-Gone is made by Dritz Corporation.

Orvus Quilt Soap is made by Quilter's Rule.

Reynolds Freezer Paper is made by Reynolds Metal Company.

Wonder Marker is made by W. H. Collins, Inc.

About the Authors

Betty Cossey has been a quilter for 18 years, and has taught her portable, wrap-around quilting technique for six years. She's made over 70 quilts, both by hand and machine, and averages three or four quilts each year. Most of these quilts now belong to her six children, 13 grandchildren and her great-granddaughter. She lived most of her life in California, and now resides in a charming, historic town in Oregon.

Lucille Harrington is the daughter of an accomplished seamstress and the granddaughter of a tailor, and she is fond of saying that she was born with tailor's chalk in her blood. She learned to sew at an early age, and her love and appreciation of fabric led her naturally to quilting. She also knits, crochets, and enjoys various forms of needlework. If it involves yarn, thread or fabric, Lucille is interested! A native of San Antonio, Texas, Lucille now lives happily in Oregon, where she and her husband, Bruce, moved after his retirement in Southern California. They are the parents of three grown sons: George, Scott and Brett.

Ordering Information

To Order by Phone

In the U.S. and Canada, call toll-free: **1.800.477.9773**

To Order by FAX

1.415.457.6718

To Order by Mail

Complete the order form and remove from the book. Mail the completed order form in an envelope, and remember to include payment (either by personal check, money order or charge card number and expiration date). Mail the order form to:

> Small Change Press
> 524 San Anselmo Avenue, #138-B
> San Anselmo, CA 94960

- All books are shipped via UPS for fast, reliable service (most shipments are received within 2–3 weeks).

- All orders must be prepaid – no C.O.D. orders.

- Payment must be in U.S. Dollars only.

- Prices are subject to change without notice.

- Our books may be available from your favorite quilt, fabric and craft stores. If you don't see them there, ask them to call Small Change Press at 1.800.477.9773.

Shipping

All books will be shipped by UPS Ground unless otherwise requested. (Most shipments are received within 2–3 weeks). In a hurry? Then we will ship by UPS Blue Label, for quick, two-day service.

Shipping Charges

	UPS Ground	UPS Blue	Canada
First Book	$4	$8	$6
Each Additional Book	$1	$2	$4

the Rose Quilts

Purchased by

Name

Organization

Street Address

City

State   Zip

Phone
(Necessary to process order)

Ship to *(if different than purchased by)*

Name

Organization

Street Address

City

State   Zip

Phone
(Necessary to process order)

Method of Payment

❏ Cash ❏ Check/Money Order

❏ MasterCard ❏ Visa   Account Number

Expiration Date

Signature

Order Information

Quantity	Title	Price Each	Total Price
	The Rose Quilts	$24.95	
	California Residents Add 8.25% Tax ($2.06/ea.)		
	Shipping/Handling (see below)		
		Total	

Shipping

All books will be shipped by UPS Ground unless otherwise requested. (Most shipments are received within 2–3 weeks). In a hurry? Then we will ship by UPS Blue Label, for quick, two-day service.

Shipping Charges

	UPS Ground	UPS Blue	Canada
First Book	$4	$8	$6
Each Additional	$1	$2	$4

Send Your Order To

Small Change Press
524 San Anselmo Avenue, Suite 138-B
San Anselmo, CA 94960

Questions? Contact us at…

1.800.477.9773/Voice
1.415.457.6718/FAX